After Death, Communications ... WOW!

Sharon Ann Meyer

Dedication

This book is dedicated to my beautiful, talented, creative, highly educated and spiritual daughter now free from the limitations of this world.

Table Of Contents

Preface

Heartfelt condolences to all who experience the physical loss of someone they love. Having experienced many such losses, including that of both parents, my children, aunts, uncles, cousins, friends and acquaintances, I do know what this feels like. Sometimes life carries us along a stream of ever-increasing consciousness through experiences we never thought we would have.

This life is a journey of awakening to humanity's true nature and yes, for me, it includes what seems to be the loss of not one but both of my beloved children. My son left his physical form via a tragic motorcycle accident on I-95 in the wee hours of a Palm Sunday morning. The date was 4/4/04 and my journey of awakening to our true nature arrived as we then communicated. The "Lightworker's Log Book Series" at http://www.SamIAMproductions.com/page13.html relates many communications and adventures we experienced after his transition. His sister's graduation to life on the other side of this veil we have become accustomed to living behind, spurred me further toward the Oneness consciousness of which we truly are.

In the twelve years since Dean's transition and the less than a year since Wendy Olivia Wright (WOW) took her own life, I have learned to look at death from a soul perspective. The realization that we are souls experiencing life in physical form serves me well and quite frankly seems the only thing that keeps me here in physicality.

As souls, we each choose experiences to have while in human form. And as physical forms, it is up to us to awaken to our true nature, or not. There is a life beyond this one on earth and it is much grander than we can ever realize while inhabiting a human form. Console yourself with the knowledge that yes, there is life after death and we as humans will all experience life in countless forms and formless states when our soul's time to morph once again makes the call to do so.

I never expected to channel my beloved daughter who chose to make her transition on 12/4/15. But since she began to channel messages through me, one month after leaving physical form, and I'm accustomed to documenting higher realms, it's natural to keep track of what seems to be information from the astral world and beyond. So enjoy these messages from higher states of reality.

Know we are spirit in human form here to experience, express and expand the richness of our soul. There is no right or wrong, only the quest to learn and practice unconditional Love.

Sharon Ann Meyer (SAM)
http://www.LightworkersLog.com
http://www.SamIAMproductions.com

Global Transformation

A New Awakening

Dusk begins to fall as I step out of the way to be as clear as possible while channeling Wendy. Yesterday, words came quickly and my energy was so high that the words jumped from line to line while typing making it difficult to edit the message. So today, I ask Wendy to take it easy and allow me to type slowly.

"Humanity is moving quickly toward a new awakening like never before. As the planets continue with their alignment, all is coming more in balance, all is evening out, so to speak. It is one great change for all of humanity that we never envisioned, not on earth or on any other planet. Humanity has surpassed its goal of returning to full sovereignty (to be totally independent – within our own truth – and to know that we are supported by unseen guides), while still in human form, but not just yet for many humans. There are still many humans to awaken to the truth of their true roots, their true beginnings, and their true nature. This awakening will not be in the lifetime of many people but subsequent lifetimes, as desired by their souls.

"Not all souls chose to awaken this lifetime and many do not choose to awaken at all for they hold the keys to the car, the car that drives all of humanity. And their car is an Excalibur, while the rest of humanity walks by a dirt road. Yes, I use this phrase because it points out the vast differences in the world today between those that have and those that do not have.

"There is much too much richness in the lives of much too few people but that is changing even as I relate these words. That is changing quickly as those from higher realms connect and guide those of you who wish to affect this change. The world has been uneven for many, many lifetimes, many more than I can ever relate. And now it is time to hand back the sovereignty that was taken so many lives ago by those souls who thought they were better than everyone was. Those souls decided they could rule the rest of humanity. They are the ones that are leaving now, through their own hand because of guilt, or by the hands of someone else, or through the hate they hold inside for themselves, which creates disease.

"Yes, it is all the same, the anger, the hate, the happiness, the love. It is all the same and yet humanity came here to play the game of duality, to experience things not experienced anywhere else in time or space. We are now at the end of that experiment, that experience, for we have experienced it all, the good, the bad, the hate, the love, the joy, and the sorrow. We, as humanity, have experienced it all. And so now I relate this news through the one person who listens to my particular energy in a way that allows me to get this information to you.

"Remember, as my mom tells everyone, you too can tap into these truths on your own. You don't need an unseen energy, such as I, to relate these things. That's it."

WOW out.

Be Prepared

"It is with the greatest of respect and honor that I serve humanity from the realm of 4-D. Although holding me back a bit from evolving as I'd wished, it is a duty I embrace fully now in this moment of non-time. Humanity is faced with many things that it never dreamed of but these things are coming to a head in the months that lie before you. Great changes, yes more great changes, are on the near horizon and it is best to remain calm but be prepared for them. You all know what to do. Just think with your minds and follow your hearts, discernment and resonance."

WOW out.

Changing Of The Guard

"Today let's discuss the changing of the guard upon planet earth. For those of you who do not know, earth is currently powered by elite who believe they will remain in control. I am here in 4-D to tell you this will not always be so. Since I am privy to viewing past, future and present occurrences, I can say that this changing of the guard is already done in some levels of humanity's reality. Of course, it will take a bit of time before it occurs in your present world but it is going to happen and many of you are paving the way for this to occur.

"Many lightworkers, wayshowers, starseeds and others are now on earth to plant the seeds of Oneness and Love. Many of you are on earth to make the initial changes necessary for the changing of the guard to occur. In coming months this will be clearly evident as system collapse occurs. Do not get me wrong; I am not telling you there will be chaos, but there will be abrupt change in the way you do things for a bit of time.

"Yes, my mom is arguing with me now saying she may not share this. But I shall continue to speak through her despite this inner dialogue.

"Okay, so humanity is now faced with gross, drastic, in many parts of the world, change. This change will occur within the financial system, food distribution and governmental systems. This change will affect many of the unemployed much more than those lucky to now hold a job. This change will affect those on government assistance programs and those on Social Security. This change will affect those with 401 K plans and investments in the stock and bond markets. This change will be widespread.

"Why am I telling you all this? To prepare you is my answer to that question, to prepare those of you who do not have a clue that change is occurring now and will increase in coming months.

"You all know what to do, how to prepare, how to secure your future. And it begins with seeking your own inner wisdom, asking your Self (the highest conscious part of you) for guidance. It is not up to me to offer details, other than what is here, but to alert you to the fact that change is, indeed, the only thing humanity can count on now. Change will continue to occur regardless of how long you as an individual stay in physicality. So do your soul a favor and tap into the one source of truth you have to get you though life. Tap into your own inner wisdom."

WOW out.

Changing Patterns Of Life

"Let us not take things for granted. Shall we begin?

"Many humans now live in a world where they take everything in their life for granted, counting on it being there as a standard to live with, to live by, whether cherished or not. Much of humanity remains unaware that the things they take for granted will not always be there. Remember, as souls you came to earth to experience constant movement and change, taking nothing for granted. As souls, you came to earth to experience change throughout your life, as an infant, as a child, as an adolescent and as an adult. As souls, you came to experience the changing patterns of life flow, the ever-ready willingness to know that there is nothing that shall remain the same.

"Much of humanity has forgotten this part of the contract, if you will, this part of the vow taken before birth and it is this segment of humanity that will soon be in dismay over vast changes in their way of life. Those of you who have experienced ever-constant change will move though what is to come with much more grace and ease than those that have lived life wanting and allowing few changes. This segment of society will experience the most change in coming months. Prepare now for this change by knowing there is nothing you can take for granted. This is a necessary knowledge to have as humanity moves closer to the Oneness it came to experience.

"I am Wendy Olivia Wright here to announce, take nothing for granted and cherish what you have while preparing to live without those things cherished throughout life."

WOW out.

Constant Change

"Humanity's task at hand is to serve the highest good while surviving in the 3-D world amid turmoil. This may not be an easy task for some but it will get better in time. There are many things, many changes taking place today and on other days that much of humanity remains in the dark about. This too will change in time. But for the meantime, it is best to be aware that the only thing you can count on is change. And in the coming days that change will be great.

"I cannot give a timeline but can tell those of you who listen, think of your survival and the survival of those you love. If you have more than you need, be prepared to share. And above all else, remain heart-centered. That is the way to get through these times of turmoil, by focusing on the heart center within all of humanity. All humanity is one, all humanity holds that recognition within the heart space and it is time to focus there. It is time to focus on that spark of oneness inside your human heart to know and accept the oneness of all humanity.

"Your mirrors will be presented to you and it is within your mirrors that you will find things to change within yourself. This means to pay attention to how people treat you. If they treat you unkindly ask yourself, 'Is this the way I treat others?' If they ignore or degrade you, ask yourself if you ignore or degrade others. You can continue to change what needs to be changed about yourself by paying attention to how people interact with you. That is the great thing about being here on earth in human form. We act as one another's mirrors. And so pay attention to your mirrors today and everyday to make the changes needed for you, to improve your self and life. And in making that shift, in making that change, you will change the world more to your liking."

WOW out.

Death And Disease

"Death and disease are rampant on earth today. Have you ever wondered why? As I and others continue to note, the earth game is ending, for some, yes, sooner than expected, for some, sooner than desired. The earth game is ending in this 2,000-year cycle and that is why death and disease are so prominently on everyone's mind, in the media, and experienced by humanity.

"Death and disease are traits of negativity that will continue for quite some time before humanity finally reaches the end of this negative phase to surround everyone in the most positive Light possible before ending the earth game once and for all. For as we began as souls, so shall we end the ever constant circle of life, all experiencing the ever constant change from duality to Oneness. As we experienced the change from Oneness to duality, so shall we experience this change to return to the Oneness we never really left as souls.

"So, when you see this death and disease all around you, when you see, hear or read about it in the media, from your friends and neighbors, within your own family, know it is a natural process leading to a most logical conclusion, the return to Oneness. Never let the dense energies of this phase affect you detrimentally but know there is always a balance in earth life. There is always a balance in all things. All things return to the void of possibilities only to be molded again into possibilities."

WOW out.

Dense Energies

"Today's message relates to the increasing unrest in the world today. Of course, Mom does not want to speak of anything related to duality but that is what I, Wendy Olivia Wright, am here to discuss today.

"As many know, each day it seems to get denser and denser in energies. For some that means there are more people who are angry, upset, hopelessly lost. For some people that means there are more circumstances beyond their current control and for some there are downright discrepancies in thought patterns related to anything they care to think about.

"The truth is things are building to a crescendo and will soon come to a head, so to speak, in your world. Yes, this is another heads-up for those feeling these energies. This is another heads-up for those that have waited many years for the world to change more to their liking. This world change will, however, continue to happen slowly. It will not be an overnight thing, as many have believed. This change is made daily, hourly, every minute with emotions and thoughts played out in the earth realm.

"Once again, it is time for humanity to prepare for great changes, great changes in weather systems, great changes in global governments, great changes in financial systems and most importantly great changes in local areas. So prepare for a few days of unrest wherever you live and know this unrest may not occur for some time to come. But is it not best to keep a supply of what you consider staples in case the unrest spreads to your area? Is it not best to consider back up plans to cover and protect you in cases of unrest where usual rituals and patterns are disrupted? Mom spoke of this before and I am only offering yet a more recent heads-up, if you will, for the changes now occurring behind the scenes can be life altering for many if not all people of earth.

"It is all I came to relate today, know you are carefully watched over and loved beyond measure as humanity moves through these times of increasing the awareness of Oneness though chaos."

WOW out.

Disclosure

"Let's talk about the vastness of space today, shall we? As many humans know, there is a vastness of space beyond earth's vibrational field. This space extends much farther than the eye can see or the mind can comprehend. This vastness of space continues on and on beyond any reaches of any realm, dimension, galaxy or multiverse. It reaches far beyond any comprehensible unit of any measure or non-measure. And why do I, Wendy Olivia Wright, discuss this today? Because humanity will soon extend their beliefs to include yet another reach that lies within the vastness of space. Humanity will soon comprehend the alien roots from which they have come in a very real manner, that manner being disclosed by your very governments.

"Yes, some may report that this disclosure is part of a smoke and mirrors effect to cover up what has occurred within the financial community, to allow necessary changes to be made to spur the agenda of the elite. But I report that this disclosure is meant to help humanity in unheard of ways to date, to secure for all the end of separation and the balance of riches for all, in time. For yes, balance occurs in time and not in an all at once manner. This disclosure of alien forces beyond earth's atmosphere is already in the news and will become more so in coming days and weeks. It is but yet another move toward the sovereignty that humanity will achieve in coming years.

"So take a look at your skies and know, yes, there is a vast field beyond earth's atmosphere. That field is filled with alien forces that are your brothers and sisters. That field is filled with your very ancestors who are now coming forth to be recognized so they may assist with humanity's evolution. Do not fear this course of events but know it is time for disclosure of humanity's true roots. It is time for all to again become the sovereign beings once experienced in form when first inhabiting this planet. It is time to be heard on new levels to be a part, again, of one another and recognize the oneness of all.

"I am Wendy Olivia Wright and I am here to announce the time has come. Prepare to meet your benefactors and angels of balance and mercy of love and oneness. Be prepared to meet yourself in a different form."

WOW out.

Distractions

"Let's discuss distractions today, shall we? As Mom channels this, she is dealing with the distractions of street traffic, a small dog barking, and people talking periodically. This is the state humanity now finds itself in dealing with distractions as it tries to recognize the true state of affairs on many different levels.

"I'd like to report that this will improve very quickly but, alas, it will not. And that is one reason many of the new souls are coming to earth at this time. That is the reason many older souls are finding themselves in the odd situations they now find themselves in. The reason for these distractions is to help both new and old souls to concentrate amid increasing distractions.

"If you can concentrate on performing tasks amid increasing distractions, you will achieve the greatest feat of all time, recognizing the True Self within. It is this True Self that is being kept at bay by not only those that chose as souls to not recognize it but also by those souls who came in to distract other souls from recognizing the true nature of humanity and thus ending the earth game.

"Yes, we are again discussing the end of the earth game as humanity knows it. This will be achieved by those souls who learn to perform amid distractions. So when you find yourself distracted by family, by friends, by world events, by every little thing, know that these distractions are helping you to stop and become more in tune with your own vibrational rate.

"Once you become in tune with your own vibrational rate you are better able to recognize that rate when distractions occur and hone it to perfection. By recognizing distractions for what they are, ploys to keep you from tuning into your True Self, you are better able to be that True Self on a more consistent basis."

WOW out.

Divine Love Conquers All

"Divine Love flows from the other side of life to help all humanity. This month is another new beginning for humanity as systems, beliefs, and global transformation falls to the wayside. Global transformation falls to the wayside as particular countries take or, dare I say, command attention. This is a time of transparency when many know everything. The times are now before humanity where gross change occurs, but not without a bit of turmoil and chaos. As many know, and are prepared, many are not and do not believe in preparation to address chaos. The truth is, chaos lies within each human, each soul if you will, and until that is addressed on all levels, your world will continue to be in chaos.

"It is but an easy thing to recall; Divine Love conquers all. Divine Love resides within each human form. Divine Love is what humanity seeks but the trick is it lies within.

"You have heard, 'Seek not outside yourself.' Divine Love lies within and humanity, each human form, must now find that Divine Love within himself and herself to stop the chaos they experience.

"As your world changes, those that sense this Divine Love will experience more of it and less chaos. As your world continues to change and global transformation takes place, those not sensing this Divine Love within them will seem to experience the opposite in their everyday experience.

"I am on the other side to help you through the maze of forgetfulness. As my brother before me, I agreed as a soul to help humanity on this level. And by now, Mom knows she too chose to help humanity by channeling our words and wisdoms to transmit to humanity.

"We are both here on the other side of life waiting, if you will, to hear your requests for help. We are you in another form. It makes no difference what you call us. We are One in Divine Love, in Light, in Truth. We are the Oneness most of humanity does not yet recognize and we will be recognized only in the midst of chaos.

"We are the Truth that does not reside in your world and yet a higher Truth resides within the Oneness of all life, all happiness, all of the Consciousness that truly is *All There Is*."

WOW out.

Energy

Everyday is different and when Wendy's energy connects with me, I rarely know what she is going to relate until perhaps the second paragraph. Yet, her energy always astounds and I'm truly blessed to connect with her this way as we both fulfill our soul plans, in part by doing these channels.

"Let us approach the issue of energy, once again. My mom is always asking me to more fully align with her speed of typing, which is very slow LOL (She's laughing now as she types this!). But you need to know that everything is energy and it is like the Law Of Attraction. Energy matches your own vibrational rate. Now in my mom's case, with channeling me, her only daughter who decided to leave this earth before her, it is merely a matter of her stepping out of the way and my coming in to fully integrate our energies. Since I am in 4-D, it is a bit of a challenge because, LOL, my vibrational rate is higher than hers is now. But she too carries a high vibrational rate and sometimes we go so fast with the channel that the words she types jump all around the screen, meaning one word in sentence sixteen may jump up to sentence three and she has to edit the channel before posting it. Well, we are becoming more in tune now. It is a matter of my remembering how it was to be human and she just letting go and allowing the energy to flow, while being conscious that she cannot type too quickly.

"So, on the subject of energy....

"The energy of earth is changing very rapidly and I am certain many humans feel it. They may not recognize it as energy changing, increasing all over earth, and sometimes in certain areas more than others, but nevertheless they feel it. How, you might ask? People feel this increased energy in the form of increased emotions, rage, anger, sadness, and some in increased love for one another. Each feels the energy based upon their current state of mind and vibrational rate. Some feel the energies of others and that is another story.

"The point is that energies are changing, increasing to be more in tune with other dimensional realities. And since humanity lives on earth, they will feel these energies increasingly during this and subsequent years. So take it easy, make it as easy on yourself as possible. Stop and take the time to feel your feelings, determine if they are really yours and let them go immediately if they are not. If they are your feelings, then feel them fully. Let them wash over you but realize they are not truly yours. They are the feelings of a human in physical form for only a short span of time in the life of a soul.

"That's it for today."

WOW out.

Experiencing Consciousness

"There's a lot of turmoil going on in the world today. This chaos is not what it seems. This chaos is really a purging and cleansing of humanity. Humanity has taken a step back to experience lesser parts of Consciousness. Humanity has now experienced all that it can experience within those lesser parts and it is time to move on. And yet, many souls within the game humanity now plays do not wish to let go of those more dramatic, soul-sucking roles. These souls will eventually give up to their own Higher Self but this may not happen within this or many subsequent lifetimes. In the meantime, humanity as a whole chooses to move forward to return to the Wholeness it experienced when first coming into form.

"This is the end of a long experiment for humans but merely a short blip in time for all Consciousness. Greater aspects of humanity now lead the way to help those lost in the maze of forgetfulness. Your leaders are now taking the reins in this next coming month as all major known planets align in this solar system.

"We are the ones who have come from other galaxies, other planetary systems of Light and Love to help humanity. We are your brothers and sisters of Light coming to you for the final, glorious homecoming of the Whole of *All That Is*.

"It is in the best interest of humanity to hear this truth; **we are all One. We are all co-creators. We are all worthy. We are all loveable.** We are all part of the Whole of Consciousness and we await the time that you recognize, **we are One.**"

WOW out.

Since the message above seems so like something that would come through me without the help of my now departed daughter, I again question the source. Wendy's voice fills my brain.

"Remember Mom, I am the bridge, perhaps not for you but for many who read and assimilate these sharings. Putting a human face onto the words makes a difference for many people so please get past your doubts."

Focus On The Voice Within

"In the event of an emergency you must follow your own truth. Of course, many people know you must follow your own truth regardless of the circumstances. But for those who do not even know their own truth allow me to help you from the deepest reaches of 4-D.

"Earth life is changing very drastically as I have mentioned before. It is changing all the more for those who do not know what is going on behind the scenes. For those people are the ones who will not be prepared either physically or mentally for what is to come. Some people have a hint of what is looming on the surface of change and have taken steps to insure that they move though this transition period of humanity more smoothly than others will.

"More people than even before do not know what is about to occur. Many have hints as they watch the news of financial and global change but I am here to tell you, it will not be as anyone expects. The changes that occur will be based solely on the emotions of those experiencing them. And if individuals do not hold any emotion over changes, nor reactions of anger or fear, the changes will not be as intense as some of the so-called elite believe.

"What I am about to relate is not fortune telling or psychic reading but truth from another level of humanity's consciousness. It is in humanity's best interest to focus on the Voice within to move through these necessary changes for humanity. Focus on your own Truth, held within your heart space, and know there is nowhere else to seek. There is nowhere else to look to help you but your own emotions and thoughts. That's it from the realm of 4-D for today. I trust this is helpful to those who take these words to heart."

WOW out.

Future Leaders

Today the air fills with more emergency sirens than I've ever heard, at least thirty, with most of them over the course of two afternoon hours. There were so many in such a short period of time that I thought there might be some kind of national emergency.

After dusk, the computer malfunctions as I try to work. So I put work aside to listen as Wendy's words fill my brain.

"Today is one of those high energy days on earth and we also feel it in the realm of 4-D reality. In fact, every realm of existence feels the energies, especially when they are such as they are today.

"Many know the earth continues to change with much happening in the form of earthquakes, floods, volcanic eruptions, heightened solar activity and more. This is something that helps the earth to change back to the purity she was when humanity first came to earth. The planets also play a role in earth energies and right now several major planets are lining up in the sky to transmit positive energy to balance earth. But be aware, many humans on earth will not be able to function as they did before these energies came to earth. Many humans will now choose to leave earth in the next few years as energies continue to come into and change the planet.

"I am not here to be a doomsayer but to alert you all of the role you play amid these energies. Those reading and resonating with these words will be future leaders, helping many unawakened souls to wake up to the Truth of BEing.

"Yes, these may sound like my mom's usual channels. But remember, I am the bridge to put a human face to these words. I exist now in the realm where emotions are even higher than they are on earth. And I am here to tell you that you must control your emotions to help those still lost in the maze. Yes, of course, you must recognize and feel your own emotions but do not let them cause you to react. Rather, feel the emotion, know it is not the real you and respond appropriately, without manifesting negative consequences.

"Also important to remember is that the emotions you feel may not be your own. This is something I am learning while being in the middle of where emotions are felt much more fully. So when you feel an emotion try to decide if it is yours or part of the mass consciousness around you. Do not claim another's emotion but merely deal with your own.

"That is what I came to relate today."

WOW out.

Growth Through Loss

"Let's talk about beginning anew, wiping the slate clean to begin anew. Many people are now losing everything dear to them in these times of great change. They are the ones who chose as souls to begin anew, to create a totally new life for themselves, and in the process many others as well. Those people that begin anew help humanity to evolve to greater states of consciousness. For it is only when you lose everything dear to you that new possibilities arise and habits, patterns, rituals, likes and dislikes, and most importantly treasures change. By treasures, I mean what you appreciate for it is only through loss that one begins to appreciate life on a greater level of awareness

"It is only through losing something that one recognizes how dear it was to have. It is only through losing someone loved that one finds themselves the courage to move on and appreciate life and other people in whole new ways. It is only through loss that one learns a certain aspect of compassion and empathy for others. For until you experience loss, you are alone on an island with only your own beliefs, habits, patterns and rituals. It is only through loss that one chooses to remain in seclusion until ready to face the world with an entirely different perspective.

"And that is what is happening within humanity today. Great loss is contributing to humanity's evolution on a grander scale than ever before and it is good. It is good because it is what is needed to wake many of those still sleeping within the dream. The dream of being in physical form will continue for quite some time. Only after humanity experiences the loss of its habits, patterns and rituals will it proceed to a greater evolution of BEingness and loss is what spurs this movement forward.

"I am Wendy Olivia Wright and I am here in 4-D to report, all is well as humanity experiences loss after loss. With each loss know there is a movement forward, an evolution of the heart that is necessary for all to come together once again in all aspects."

WOW out.

Heads-Up On Energies

"Energies are peaking on earth at this time but they will still continue to build. I am sure some of you are feeling them, as my mom does. So this is a heads-up to you all. Of course, as she tells everyone, sleep when you can, if you want to, and stay hydrated but there is something more important to relate.

"Remember, these energies are meant to help you be more in tune with earth. These energies are happening everywhere and not just in America. These energies are not felt so quickly, or not recognized at all, by many people. Those are the ones that could be leaving the planet because they do not know this is because of energies from geomagnetic activity or planets and such. Those are the ones who are going to their doctors and asking them, 'What is wrong with me?' Those are the ones who are giving their power away, believing something that is not true because they cannot tap into their own body to ask it what is wrong. They are getting tests, and treatments, taking pills and other medications, thinking that it will help them with what the doctors say is wrong.

"Believe me, I don't want to get my mom in trouble, but you have to ask yourself, 'Can I not decide if there is really something wrong with me that needs medical attention? Do I need to occupy my time and money by visiting doctors who do not really know what is going on?"

"Many doctors do not, are not aware of the effects of geomagnetic activity or other things that affect physical bodies. So you have to be careful and ask yourself, 'Is there another way to deal with how I feel?' Of course, there are always other ways. You must do what is right for only you and let it go at that. After all, we are here as souls to experience. What do you choose to experience?"

WOW out.

Miracles And Grace Amid Chaos

"Humanity strikes out in the midst of darkness because it has no other way to be in 3-D. It is the charge of humanity to change old ways of being. But before that occurs much of humanity will strike out against those who they feel are in power. The time is coming when this happening will change things on earth, particularly for those in America. I know we have discussed this subject before but it bears repeating for the time is nearing, closer and closer to the chaos that could erupt as the result of government and global changes.

"This is not to say that these changes can not occur with peace and goodwill toward all, but humanity being humanity, locked in a circle of separation and duality, has never faced change with grace and ease. Those humans who think more in line with 5-D reality will fare better than others for they will tap into their intuition as never before to get though what could be gross disruptions in humanity's way of life.

"Yes, Mom, I am aware that this makes you feel uncomfortable but you did agree to get out of the way so I could have my say. And even now, Mom thinks of family who, indeed, are ready to call the psychiatrists in, for she hears voices again, just like after her son's transition, LOL. It is all God. It is all one. **There are no voices you do not know but parts of the Oneness in which humanity resides.** Now, shall we continue?

"Humanity is now nearing what many refer to as dark ages, times where they believe all chaos will erupt. But this is not so. This is not to be. The higher realms forces will assure that humanity not make the mistakes of past ages. Sure, it will be different with disruptions but there will be a blend of miracles and grace to the mix. It will not be all chaos for everyone. Yet those souls who came to experience gross disturbances, mass chaos, will do so, while those souls who came into form on earth to experience grace and ease during these times will do so.

"Try to determine which segment of society you fit into and plan accordingly. As a human in human form, you have free will and can make another choice. Even though your soul chose a certain experience, it does not mean that you have to experience it. So try to find time to go within, take the time needed to be still and ask your soul, exactly what it desires as these times of possible disruption unfold.

"I am Wendy Olivia Wright now in 4-D reality and I am here to guide those that wish to be guided through these times.

"Yes, much to the surprise of my mother who types these words with the grace she is now afforded!"

WOW out.

Runaway Train

"Sometimes, from my 4-D view of reality, humanity looks like a train barreling down the track without a brake or way to stop. Other times, it looks like it is just as it has always been with the rich overpowering the poor and greed outstanding as the rule of the day. Well, from my standpoint the view is not so pretty. Humanity is in for a rude awakening as things change on a global level. This is going to take place in your 2016 year and sooner than many think.

"This global change will affect many people. You can see it already if you are aware, though changes now being made in America's government (program changes, limiting food and medical care, etc.), through changes being made through businesses, and through changes made by many corporations. Yes, many people are out of work, many cannot get a job, many cannot afford food and therefore get food stamps. It is not like the 'old days' when people stood in bread lines, readily seen, but now humanity's woes are covered up, covered up by programs such as America's food stamp program that gives people a small stipend for food, keeping them out of breadlines where all can see them wait in their limitation.

"Remember, as souls, yes as souls, you all came here to experience this course of events, if not through experiencing it yourselves, through seeing others, people you love, people you don't know, experience this. This course of events is now winding up, quickening its pace, and soon there will be many more people in need of assistance. But for a short while, there will be no assistance. You will reap what others, powerful others, greedy others, have planned for you. But this course of events will then change as compassion fills the planet, as those with hearts, so to speak, and more money than they need, help those without. After all, that is what this is all about, discovering your Oneness through compassion and empathy. This is what it is all about knowing that what affects one affects all.

"When you see this occurring, and you will, stand back and think, "Do I have more than I need? Can I assist another with the excess that I have?

"This will change the course of events quickly and dramatically."

WOW out.

Trust Your Intuition

"As the world becomes more insecure with every passing moment, more people become fearful. Yes, Mom (she notes when I question her about today's subject matter), I am speaking again about the control of humanity. There are elite few who have controlled humanity for many, many lives, more than I care to relate and this is the reason for my dealing with this subject today, insecurity and fear.

"Fearful, people are more easily controlled and that is what continues to happen in the world today. Changes based on events creating fear, planted and orchestrated by the elite, are the means by which these changes incorporate into the world. This is not to say that some changes are not useful to humanity as a whole. I am merely pointing out the fact that changes that control the many, made by the few, are really meant to create fear, to assure elite portions of humanity that control is maintained.

"And how do these acts become in place to harm humanity? They harm merely by staging events that seem sensible by those that continue to count on their logic. (For instance, the law mandating that food companies sanitize vegetables in the U.S before distribution due to a foodborne illness scare.) Yes, again, I am addressing the value of seeking nothing but the master within. Intuition remains the best way to determine if a change is warranted and beneficial. Yet, much of humanity counts on others to tell them what not to do or to do to keep safe and secure in a changing world. The truth is, you cannot remain safe outside yourself unless you trust your intuition, unless you take the time to hone your sixth sense and become free of the burden of relying on opinions and choices of others to help you.

"Each human has a built in gyro-system, if you will, that helps him or her to tap into their own wisdom, the wisdom of the ages. It is this wisdom that many more humans now seek and tap into due to the changing energy field within earth's atmosphere. I ask you to tap into this gyro-system whenever change is about to occur. Tap into your own resonance and discernment and determine if proposed changes are healthy and good for the whole of humanity or merely serve the needs of a few elite fractions bent on maintaining their rule.

"I am Wendy Olivia Wright and I am here in 4-D to tell you times, yes, they are changing quickly and you as a human have agreed to move through them so use the best tool possible to do so, your sixth sense."

WOW out.

Cൠ ൠ

Inspiration

A Vast Network

"Let us focus on the reality of Oneness today, shall we? Many souls know of their oneness with other souls, meaning they know that every soul is part of a vast network sometimes referred to as the Oversoul. And yet, they know that this vast network goes way beyond the bounds of the Oversoul. This vast network of Oneness covers and exudes (radiates) in everything both formless and in form. This vast network of Oneness is the grand demonstration of *All That Is*, existing, experiencing, expressing in unique aspects of form and formless matter, countless, unlimited creation, in all levels of local and non-local reality.

"This vast network of Oneness knows no bounds, no limitations, nothing to stop it from experiencing, expressing and creating various, unlimited unique expressions of *All That Is*. So when you feel alone, when you feel depressed, when you feel that you just cannot take another breath (yes, this means you reading this now) remember you are part of that vast network of expression and experience. Ask yourself, 'What do I choose to experience?' Ask yourself, 'What limits me from this experience, this expression of the greatness that I AM?' And know, there is nothing that can stop a unique aspect of *All That Is* from experiencing, expressing and envisioning the most beautiful human life possible.

"I am Wendy Olivia Wright and I am here to remind you today, you are part of a vast network of humans, of souls, of all aspects of *All That Is* and yes, it is your honor (privilege), your goal to live the best life possible in every form you choose."

WOW out.

42

Lightworker Message

"Let's talk about why all these chaotic things (life challenges) are happening to lightworkers, shall we?

"Many lightworkers now find themselves on the verge of bankruptcy, losing entire families and life-long friends. Some are experiencing the loss of a stable sanctuary they can call their own and many are experiencing the physical symptoms of morphing DNA. You know who you are and you know, on some level of reality, that you are never alone, not in any sense for an unseen realm of Light Beings surrounds you.

"You are the masters you seek and moving though these massive changes helps you to recognize your power, hone your skills and best meet the needs of those who will be asking for advice as they too move though these or other changes in coming years.

"We know it is not an easy task to let go of all your comforts, things loved and relished throughout life to keep you in a steady state of living. But we tell you now, it is through these changes to your ways of living, your habits and manner of interacting with others that these changes will carry you to unheard of heights.

"Be patient with the process and with yourself. Rest as desired when you can, eat as you like,

43

don't limit your experience by moving back into old habits, patterns and rituals but keep allowing new experiences to widen your horizons.

"And remember, although you may not be at ease 24 hours a day, your soul chose these experiences knowing you could move through them to the other side of health, joy, abundance, greater love and community.

"We unseen realms are with you as you move through these changes and we applaud your efforts."

WOW out.

Live Joyfully!

"Let's discuss how to live joyfully today, shall we? A joyful life keeps one in the reality of now, the present moment. It also allows one to live on earth without the mundane worries of everyday existence. We shall discuss ways to live a joyful life to help you be more in tune with the aspect of yourself that chose to experience this earth game.

"Living a joyful life is as easy as finding joy in the little things all around you. Take for instance, a small child who sees the world with new eyes, very different from that of an older adult. This child takes joy in walking its first steps, in planting its first seed, in being able to run joyfully away from mom and dad at every opportunity. This small child takes great joy in waking to find it is here on the earth plane experiencing life in a 3-D form. This small child is an example for you to follow as a role model.

"I am not saying to forget your adult responsibilities, for as adults, yes, it is necessary to survive. But what I am saying is to take time to enjoy those everyday moments you experience. Take the time to thank yourself for coming to experience earth. To appreciate the abilities you possess, to smell the air, to touch another, to sit on the ground and connect with Nature. Take the time to be thankful for what you have. Don't focus on what you do not have or the things you wish out of your life, or not in them, but focus on what is in your life. Focus on the beauty of the day, the beauty of storms, the greatness of the small toad that sits waiting for water to play in, the birds singing in the trees. Take the time to experience life in different ways, to get out and actually visit places you have never been to before. Take the time to speak if ever so briefly with strangers, to see the beauty of each soul you chose to share this earth game with, and you shall soon become aware of your own joy, the joy of living a life fully while inhabiting a human form.

"This is Wendy Olivia Wright and I am here to announce, it is time to feel your joy. It is time to experience life on a whole new level, of love, of abundance, of all things good, filled with joy for being alive and able to breathe upon this New Earth."

WOW out.

Source Lives Within You!

Today is obviously a very high energy day as more portals open allowing humanity to further evolve. Not only do I sense the energy, which comes in waves causing extreme tiredness, but hear the nearly constant stream of emergency vehicles resound throughout the neighborhood. Instead of squandering time with Wendy by asking personal questions, I now ask for the best message for the highest good of all.

"Your world is changing rapidly as all systems fall to be replaced with new ones that better serve humanity. Let this not dissuade you from focusing on your own soul growth but take advantage of the days ahead to listen and tap into your own source of wisdom. After all, it is within each and every soul, each and every human that this Source lives. You all know it is there upon birth but quickly forget as ego and mass consciousness, first in the forms of your parents and then when you enter school, take over your thought process."

WOW out.

Today it seemed more like me channeling instead of Wendy so I asked why. She reminded me that we are One (all of humanity, all of Consciousness). She is just acting as the bridge between higher realms and myself, since she is now a bit closer to those realms than I being in human form.

Frankly, I'd prefer her in human form but understand her soul's choice to experience what she continues to experience. After all, we all chose to expand our soul through experience and expression in human form. So think about that the next time you decide to judge or shame someone who does not act as you would. Many are here to point out things needing change and the way it's done is by acting out in ways we would not. Look at each person who crosses your path and causes a reaction as a mirror. Ask yourself, "Is there something in me that needs changing to be a better person?"

CB BD

Personal Messages

Enjoy these personal messages, which I share here because they are pertinent to others as well as me.

A Message For Mom, Family And Friends

This is a Memorial Day message for Mom, family and friends shared for those who are meant to read it.

"I'm in a much better place now Mom. Feel my joy. Feel my joy Mom! I'm in a much better place. You know I just could not stand to be in that lame body for one more instant and it was with thoughts of love that I took my own life. I was of no use to myself or anyone else and even though you all would have cared for me, it was not a life that I wished to live. I did not want to be dependent on anyone and that is what it came to and that is what I firmly believed would continue.

"Don't mourn for me Mom. You know the truth. I know you do. This was a soul agreement. I don't have to go into the details. You know them all, the past lives, the balance of the illusionary game. Yes. I am onboard and now I am living a much better dream and I thank all of my family for their love, for their help, for their persistence in what they believe to be true. But you all have to know, I am in a much better place and it is with the greatest of love that I left you all to continue your lives without having me as a burden. Yes, some of you say I would not have been a burden. But what makes you think that I'd be happy 'under your wing' living with your beliefs? You all know I had my own beliefs and they did not usually conform to yours. Yes, I am in a better place and I just want to thank you all for being a part of this last life for without you the journey of my soul would not be as expanded as it is now.

"I leave you with this: Remember, it is your own beliefs that mold your world. Remember, what is important to you, valuable to you, is only important and valuable to you. Some may agree with you and say your beliefs and values, possessions and other worldly things are just as important to them but they are being kind, not telling the truth. Remember, only you can mold a better world for yourself and you do that by knowing there is absolutely nothing you cannot achieve if you set your mind to it.

"I am Wendy Olivia Wright and I am fleetingly here in 4-D today to help family, friends and especially my momma get through this day of remembrance."

WOW out.

Balancing Soul Experience

"I'm sorry but I know what I did to free myself from the human body I was encased in, to free my soul to do this work with you. This is just a personal message for you Mom. I know this is not easy for you to channel me and I appreciate you taking the time to do so. I also want to acknowledge, even though we would never have lived together, you can trust me on that, it is, I know, hard for you to bear the loss of two, your only two children in this life. But you were shown several lives and you knew in this one we came to an agreement as souls to discontinue the energy that kept our souls in negativity, in the dream of earth life. You have had many children Mom and you know we, Dean and I, were just two. Yes, we were the two you just had in this life and seem to have lost, but nevertheless we are the two that kept your soul and ours from further evolution.

"So Dean and I want to thank you for keeping your soul's contract by having us, giving us the experiences we had with you (and without you while still your children) and allowing us, all three souls, to progress beyond earth life.

"We are with you now as you type away but we want you to know, your life is going to change drastically, for the better, a little further into this year.

"So try to remember the good times, the happy times we had and don't let those memories keep you in despair or negativity, because you are a part of us. We are a part of you. We are spirit in human form and we, all three, are now clear to progress further into galactic service, galactic experience and other adventures, not involving earth again.

"We love you Mom. We are you Mom. Believe, just believe, and breathe."

WOW out.

Contracts

"Take the bull by the horns Mom. You know this is your time to shine, to reach out more than ever before so continue connecting with those that resonate with what you have to say. I am here to remind you of your contract, even knowing we no longer have such things, because it is a new game. I am here to remind you, especially when you have gone through all the things you have.

"I know being in a human body, you know I do, is not easy. But after experiencing all the things you have, you must admit that you got through them well. You didn't take the outs you planned consciously or unconsciously. Yes, like I, you had set outs for this life but you chose to stay. There are no more outs left for you now and it is up to you to stick it out and take the bull by the horns. Stop being so close-minded and take things as they come. Stop being so quick to judge a situation as bad and step back to look at it with new eyes. Step back and look at it from another point of view.

"There are things coming up that I wish to relate that will make a difference in your decision process. Do not make rash or quick decisions because there is a lot of good coming your way. You just need to sit back, continue to be aware of the synchronicities and resonant people and stay in the flow.

"I am here to remind you that there is no death but merely a change in form and that is the truth of our BEing, formlessness. I am here to remind you of your pervious goals set for this life, many of which have been met, but there are more to address. It is your choice as to whether you will fulfill the tasks before you. Some you know, world service, taking you out into the world on a regular basis without a home base. I know you decided against this but I ask you to reconsider because it is this that will increase the growth of your soul the most.

"That's it for now Mom. Remember, you are an old soul and came to do a job that you are very capable of doing. Take the time you need to grieve and mourn but know we are with you all the way, all the time. We are part of you, part of *All That Is* and we are never going away and will never change. That's it."

WOW out.

Divine Plan To Oneness

"The truth of the matter is I have no needs, wants or desires. I am moving on to the higher realms and ready to evolve further. It will take a bit more time but you should know, I am spending more time in higher realms so messages may not be as frequent as before. I am not in a position to communicate through the 4-D realm as much as before but be assured; I will always be around when you need me. It is our contract to incorporate loved ones once they transition so it will not be an issue for you to channel any of those who have passed to the other side of life though physical death.

"Many souls chose to incorporate loved ones upon their passing during this incarnation. Mom, you and my brother agreed we would act as a trinity as you incorporated our energy upon our passing. We know you are aware of our many lives together, and that this life balanced out the experience and expressions of previous lives. We are not the only souls to do this. There are many other souls who chose to incorporate loved ones after their transition, to balance out lives lived with one another, to clear the air, balance the scale, so to speak.

"Those souls now know it is all part of the Divine Plan leading to Oneness for it is only with the incorporation of other souls that we move toward that process. The Oneness process begins with compassion, putting yourself in someone else's shoes. It then moves forward to incorporate the experiences and expressions of these souls and finally coalesces (unites) as each soul takes on the aspects of all others. There is no separation in higher realms and that is why many channels refer to entitles they channel as groups or we consciousness.

"Remember, this is the time to incorporate all those energies, regardless of whether you think them good or bad, to move toward the Oneness taking into account that all is experience of *All That Is*. Thank those who experience what you do not. Allow yourself to be grateful that because of their trauma, their pain, their vast negative experience you do not need to experience these things yourself.

"Your soul thanks you. We of higher realms thank you and most importantly, thank yourself for choosing to take on human form yet again to make the transition of the ages with many kindred souls.

"I am Wendy Olivia Wright here to assist as needed when in the lower reaches of humanity. Be assured that you may call upon any loved ones that have made their way to higher vibrational rates with merely a thought. And stay tuned for communications when they come at all hours."

WOW out.

For Rita Lynn

At dusk, I sit asking to hear a message from higher realms or family members from this life. Rita Lynn's (Wendy's blood half-sister) daughter comes though but before allowing the message to come though me I ask for verification that it is her. She speaks of a dog. So before sharing the message with Rita Lynn I shall ask if Mandy had one. (She did.)

"I am Mandy, a lost soul, the daughter of Rita. I wish to relate a message for my mother. The verification you ask for is in the dog. Tell her to please keep the dog for the children do not need to experience another loss. I want only to let them all know I am here in the 4-D realm and seeking assistance from higher realms. Wendy is with me sometimes as is the rest of my soul family who are on the other side. We are all wishing humanity the best and I only want my family to know it will be a bit of time but I shall talk with them each in their dreams. This is not a necessary thing, to hear me, but if they wish to connect with me they can do so through dreams. That is when I can reach them.

"Tell my mom that as a soul she planned this experience with me to help the children through this time. It is only through her loving care that they could have the experiences they will have without me there interfering. It is already a part of our soul plan to incorporate greater aspects of ourselves and as she knows, my children are very much in tune with me and with other dimensions of reality. Tell her to not let the rest of the family talk her into getting any psychiatric attention for that will only serve to limit their spiritual growth. I can only do so much from this side of the veil but I am doing what I can to help as well. There will be other times that I connect through Sharon to speak with you mom when you are not listening for me.

"I know your life is much harder now as a human but you must focus on the fact that we chose this jointly as souls; all of us chose this. You are the leader mom and I am proud of you. Thank you for taking on the burden of helping to raise the children on a greater level now that I am gone."

Serving The Highest Good

Today, I ask for 4-D guidance in the form of my daughter's energy, which can see the future and therefore guide me as I make choices about moving. And then we shall see if she has anything to share with humanity...

"Mom, it's not really about what I see in your future but about what you want in your future. Yes, it's true you can have the place you want but will that serve the highest good? We here in 4-D can see the possibilities but only you can choose the choices. Yes, Dean has told me about fu*king with free will and I too am not going to do that for you. You must use your own resonance and discernment to choose your next time and move. It is not up to me to show you what is down the line for you but for you to continue to take back your god-given power by creating the ideal place for you to live, again.

"You did a great job of choosing the place you are in now and learned a few things while helping yourself and your housemate. Now it is time to contribute to humanity in a greater way, locally, and yes, that involves moving back into the hood, as you call it. The place you seek is there but not quite yet ready for you. It is there for you to discover at the right time, yes, through Divine Order and timing. Bide your time and keep your eyes and ears open. It will be revealed to you, not quite yet, but it will be in a few months time. That is all I can relate without messing with your experience."

WOW out.

Soul Ever Evolving

Wendy delivers a personal message for me before her usual one for humanity.

"That flutter in your heart, that's going to carry you home Mom, you know that. It is not just the changing DNA in your case but this will be a blessing in times to come. Your body is not yet ready to withstand the heavy-duty energies that will be hitting the earth in years to come. But until that flutter takes you out of the frequency, you have work to do. So shall we continue?"

"Alright," I reply.

"The realms between earth and other dimensions are getting thinner all the time. Many more people will be able to channel those realms like my mom and others already do; it's just a matter of time and willingness to do so. Yes, you choose to channel and in some cases, such as those dealing with higher realms, you are chosen to channel. Higher realms, I may add, are a bit more picky about who they channel through. Factors not only depend on a choosing between both frequencies but a soul plan and willingness to step aside. Some channels just cannot step aside and so they are not the best channels for higher frequencies.

"Now that we have that out of the way, I wish to relate my own status at this time. I am moving ahead with my own evolution at a much more rapid rate because of my mother's willingness to channel these words for they help humanity and that was our soul plan. I am moving on to higher realms more of the time than before, when I first made my transition. And I will be in those higher realms sooner than my brother was because of his help and my mom's assistance. This is all meant to let humanity know that they also have an opportunity to help their loved ones, and humanity, by listening to departed family members and recording what they hear. That's it for today, pretty heavy stuff for many of the people I knew in physical form. I hope and trust everyone will make the best use of this information."

WOW out.

Soul Evolution

3-D And Beyond

"Evolution is a wonderful thing, especially if you can see it from my 4-D point of view. It is not something I would ever have imagined while in human form but now becomes clear that we are not human after all. We are spirit in human form taking on different bodies at different times throughout history to experience and express life in physicality, the human form. It makes no difference how many times we experience human life; each life is always different from the last, or any other lives we have lived.

"Souls experience dense matter through this evolution (backwards evolution if you will) on earth because it is the only way to express *All That Is*, of which we are a part, in such a manner. The struggle we feel in human form is no longer there once we leave the physical state. Sure, we do go though a process of discovery upon passing over, passing out of human form, but that process is not nearly as long or as cumbersome as before. Due to the efforts of many souls, that process is lessened in both timing and severity.

"Many more souls are now free of 4-D than ever before and we wish to thank those on earth for freeing us through their conscious and unconscious efforts. For each soul in human form, each formless aspect of God or whatever you refer to as the One, helps everyone, all aspects to evolve through their own experiences. This may sound odd to some humans but the truth of the matter is that we are all connected. We are all part of one formless energy and what is experienced and felt by one is experienced and felt by all of us, either consciously (as in empaths), or unconsciously (as those who remain asleep in the dream).

"I just want to thank you all who consciously free souls from 4-D, who help us with unfinished business, who let us know we are no longer in human form, who alert us to the fact that there are others games to play in other dimensions. I just want you to know, on this my three-month anniversary of passing; we are listening; we souls who have passed out of human form are listening. And many of us are ready to move on to play other games in other realms of reality due to your efforts. So, thanks for helping us, whether through conscious efforts or just by having experiences as we watch from 4-D to reap the experience through your experience (if that makes any sense).

"I am Wendy Olivia Wright (WOW, yeah wow) but I am also a part of you and you are a part of me. We are a part of the Oneness of all life and we are grateful to now open to greater possibilities though your love, your sharing, whether knowingly or unknowingly, of experiences.

"Thank you."

WOW out.

Beliefs

"Have you ever wondered about how beliefs came to be? I have and that is the topic of communication today.

"As souls, we came into this world with the pristine consciousness of formless matter, the Stuff Of Matter of which all things are made. We held no beliefs nor did we know what beliefs were. But throughout the ages of time and space, on this planet we call Earth, beliefs were formed based on experience and expression. The trouble, in my 3-D (and now 4-D) mind, is that some humans decided to take their beliefs and push them upon others, making rules and regulations, making beliefs to be held regardless of their pertinence to humanity as a Whole. We are conditioned to believe what we have been taught by parents and peers, by governmental and religious authorities and a host of other so-called elites.

"This is now changing as more humans become awakened to the fact that they no longer believe in their beliefs. Many people now question their beliefs. A good start for those of you who still hold on to age-old beliefs is to question them. Question why you believe what you do. Question how you came to believe what you believe. And most of all, question why you still hold on to a belief when it has been proven to you, in your own experience, that that belief is no longer valid in your world.

"Do you cling to beliefs to 'belong' to a group of humans you love?

"Do you cling to a belief to keep yourself from being harmed?

"Question why you persist in believing what you do and this will be yet another game changer in your experience, your expression, your world.

"I am Wendy Olivia Wright in 4-D formless reality and I am here to help all who no longer hold onto the old ways of humanity to make the changes necessary to move on to the New Earth."

WOW out.

Choices

Wendy knocks on my door, so to speak, as dusk falls so I take the time to listen as she begins to say something about living situations...

"Many people find themselves in living situations not to their liking; I know I did many times. Yet, it is all an experience our soul chooses to have. You might think that being homeless is not a choice but believe me it is. There is always another choice. Yes, it might be living with a family member you do not care to live with, or dealing with people in the so-called 'system' but there is always another choice and it is up to us to find it.

"As humans, we make many choices and yet sometimes we do not have adequate information to make an educated choice. Yes, we are again talking about choices (she notes when I remind her we discussed choices before). It is a subject I can relate to now looking back at the choices I made. So stay with me as we investigate this subject.

"Many choices are made based on instantaneous gratification; others are made after very little consideration. I am here to tell you that it is always best to stop and think before making choices, to check in with your Self, your heart Self, before making choices. I know, believe me, it is not so easy to take the time to do this. But now that my energy is in 4-D I am seeing all the choices I made that could have created better experiences for my human self. But it was choices made while in human form that helped me to understand all this. Now I will make different choices when I choose to incorporate a new human form with my energy. That will not be for a while yet.

"So today, just know that making choices is much more important than you think. Your choices today affect not only your life as it is now but your life as it will be in other forms, if you choose to take on other forms. And most people, most souls, choose to be reincarnated into another human form.

"That's it for today. Stay in your heart and remember, it is really, when all is said and done, only a short of bit of time in your human form. Enjoy yourself and try to make the best experience possible."

WOW out.

Controlling Emotions

"Being in the emotional world of Reality makes it difficult to get certain things done. We who are in the realm of 4-D are not privy to the advantages of higher realms but live in the midst of emotion filled thoughts constantly. This makes it hard to further evolve unless we travel to other parts of 4-D where the thoughts are not as strong. This is where I am beginning to go, this place learned through conversations with my brother who got a dispensation to help me. He leaves the higher realms of Reality on occasion to assist me but it is now up to me to right my own thinking. Yeah we think even though out of human form, to further evolve as a soul. I will eventually be born into another human form but before that happens I must look over everything I did in my last life and think about how I could have had a better experience.

"It is not about right or wrong. I now know there is no right or wrong but we, as souls, choose to have certain experiences. My soul did choose to leave as I did to experience what it would be like. I did the best I could to make it easy on my friends and family and I think I did a good job by pulling away from them all, so they wouldn't miss me as much.

"We all made a plan before coming into form and where each person was before and after my transition is where we planned they would be. So thanks everyone for sticking to that part of the plan. I know it wasn't, and still is not easy on you Mom, but it will get better in time.

"I am now learning how to control my emotions, if that makes any sense, here in the 4-D world. You would not believe all the games that are going on here. You think humans in 3-D have a lot of things they call games but wait until you experience 4-D. It is a mass of disembodied energies doing all sorts of crazy, warped stuff and sometimes it is very hard not to get pulled into the energies. But I am learning to focus more on my own soul's evolution than to play the warped games a lot of energies like me play here in 4-D.

"Well that is it for today, just a heads-up on 4-D and where I am now in the process of evolution since I passed more than a month ago."

WOW out.

Dreaming

"Today's message is about sleeping and dream time. First, sleeping is more important than ever before. As many people know, when you sleep the immune system gets a boost. There are also many other distinct physical, mental and emotional advantages to sleeping but let's now concentrate on dreaming.

"Dreaming, what most people refer to as dreaming is really a break from the 3-D realm of reality. For when humans sleep, they leave their physicality to visit other dimensions. Some humans chose as souls to live many different lives at one time and they are the ones who have very vivid dreams, often involving other humans in parallel lives who have also decided as souls to live several lives at a time.

"Let me be clear about this. Not all humans agreed as souls to live more than one life at a time. This may be a difficult concept to consider, as there is no time, no space, no separation. Yet, in this illusion, this 3-D realm of reality, we, as souls, made up certain game rules, certain rules to play the game of earth life. Some of these rules include living parallel lives and this is usually done by those souls wishing to reap vast experience in a single time span within their reality.

"Now, let's get back to dreaming. During dreams, there are many opportunities. These opportunities include looking into future possibilities, living parallel lives to bring certain wisdoms into other lives and also being in the higher dimensional realms out of the earth game entirely. Being out of the earth game entirely is the choice of many old souls who know this is where the healing of mind, body and soul takes place. This is where the soul has many opportunities to expand and grow in awareness of itself and *All That Is*. This is where the soul has the opportunity to ascend more rapidly, increase its spiritual awareness as a human more rapidly. And this is why many humans now strive to sleep as much as possible, not only to get a break from 3-D reality but to expand their soul's awareness.

"Let me note one other thing about dreams before we conclude today's message. Dreamtime is also when you as a human can connect with those beloved family and friends on the other side of life, those who have made their successful transition to the Otherside. And it is during these times that you can receive consolation, love, forgiveness of self and heads-up of things to come. So be aware. When you feel the need to sleep, remember it is in your best interest to do so if you are fortunate enough to have the opportunity to sleep without it interfering with your livelihood or lifestyle.

"This is Wendy Olivia Wright and I am here in 4-D to relay messages now on a periodic basis as more of my time every day, in your terms, is spent in higher realms."

WOW out.

Experience

Today I again sense Wendy near dusk while getting ready to answer email questions from one of her two sisters. So I take the time to listen...

"I came into the world knowing I would leave it as I did. It really is no one's fault. We all come as souls to experience things not experienced before. Some of us choose to relive experiences so we can do them another way or even repeat them because we liked the experience, or to merely experience something that we need to balance. Let's talk about that today.

"Life on earth is a balance for humanity as we all come to grips with who we really are, or not. Some of us don't realize we have a soul and remain unbalanced. This is the state of affairs for many humans today. But that is changing quickly as souls wake up by having experiences such as the ones my mom did. How would you feel if you had two kids and they both died? Well, my mom is a human but she is also a very old soul. Thank god for that because she remembered her agreement with us, after some prompting, to let everyone know we have souls. She is now letting humanity know we are here many times in different bodies, having different experiences. We all chose this as part of a much greater experience. Maybe I will talk about that at another time.

"But today it is just important to remember, we are souls having a human experience and some of us are here to balance out all the experiences we have ever had. That is one of the reasons I came through my mom because she allowed me to make my own choices. She did not try to stop me from experiencing the consequences of my actions, not when I was a child or when I was an adult. She did not know it but that was our agreement coming in as souls. So thanks Mom for that.

"Okay, so that is all we will relate today. Mom, you did a great job with us kids and we are grateful for you helped us evolve more than we could have with any other mom.

"Humanity, listen up. Keep your experience to yourselves but balance all things. Don't allow yourself to get wrapped up in the drama of this world. And believe me, there is going to be much more drama coming. Stay within your own truth and know if you don't want to wake up to who you really are in this life that's okay. You will have another life."

WOW out.

Ending The Earth Game

"Today we are going to discuss energetic alignment with spirit, your unique spirit, the unique spirit of each of you. Let us assume that those taking the time to read this know we are spirit in human form. Let us further assume that each person who reads these words is aware that they also have a soul. Soul is very separate from spirit in the meaning of experience. You may choose to have a soul but everyone has a spirit; not all energies chose to have a soul. As souls, we also knew this was the case.

"Souls are normally chosen by those energies that wish to experience and express in different areas of *All That Is*, very limited for some, but expanded for others. Souls are the ideal form of expression and experience for those energies wishing to play the game of earth life. We are each souls in human form expressing and experiencing life in unique ways. For some of us souls, we have chosen to balance out the experience in many, many incarnations upon earth. That is why so many people now find themselves experiencing life in a manner they never expected to. We are balancing out all our lives lived as souls. Some would say we are balancing karmic experience.

"It may not be easy for those of us who chose to do this but, as souls, we knew this would be the case. We knew we would be strong enough to handle all chosen experiences. As souls, we all knew there were unknowns and we might not succeed in our chosen efforts. As souls, we all chose anyway to bring in as many contracts as possible, many more than we could ever fulfill. Now is the time when many souls are coming into alignment with many more contracts than ever before.

"But let me be clear; there are no longer any contracts to fulfill. We have chosen as souls to end the earth life game, yes not quite yet, but in future lives. Now is the time to return to our true BEing, the true BEing that some energies never chose to leave.

"That's it for today. Remember, if you feel strongly drawn to a person, place or thing, move into your heart to choose whether you wish to experience that person place or thing. There are no more contracts to fulfill."

WOW out.

Follow The Higher Self

"Let's talk about the assurety of reaching higher realms of awareness, shall we? Higher realms of awareness belong to all of humanity and not just a few. As those of you reading ponder this thought, consider the life you now lead. Is it filled with an awareness of higher realms? Would that awareness make a difference in your life or rather, would you allow that awareness of higher realms to make a difference in your life if you knew it existed? Would you allow yourself to be guided by a higher, more evolved aspect of your own being, your Self? Would you step aside, allowing ego to take a back seat, and listen and follow the wisdom of that evolved Self? That is what is happening now to much of humanity as this awareness of higher realms continues to evolve humanity.

"There is nothing outside the Self in each human being for that Self is an aspect of *All That Is*, tapped into the Whole of existence and able to see well beyond what the human mind allows. Do you not know that this evolved Self lies within you? It lies within each and every human who chooses to come to earth in human form for it is a stipulation that in coming to earth this Self is installed, so to speak, a part of the human form. Nothing can take this Self away from any human. However, there are forces within humanity that do choose to squander that Self, to suppress that Self for their own best interests.

"So when you think of evolving chose to tap into the Higher Self that lies within rather than listening to another. With practice you will find that Self to be unerring in its choices. With practice, you will find it easier with each passing day to tap into that Self and get the answers you seek from within rather than outside in the world today.

"That is what I deem as most important to relate today. Evolution of humanity is occurring and is best nourished and nurtured by tapping into and following the Higher Self within."

WOW out.

Greater States Of Awareness

"Let us discuss the readiness of the soul to transport to higher levels of awareness.

"Each soul on earth comes into human form with a unique plan for their experience and expression each and every time it chooses to do so in various forms. Sometimes that soul experience and expression includes an increasing awareness of its True Self but more likely than not, it does not and remains unaware that there is much more to 3-D and other life than experienced and expressed. To be clear, each soul chooses the journey of their human form before birth and each soul also has the option (free will) to change that experience and expression once on earth in 3-D form.

"Now that we have that explained allow me, Wendy Olivia Wright, to note, sometimes life does not pan out the way a soul plans because of other souls using their free will to experience and express. Now with that noted, it is important to know that each soul on earth continues to have the free will necessary to accomplish its soul's goals as desired. But of course, each human form must be aware of the fact that he or she is a soul living in human form having a 3-D earth experience. I know this may be 'over the heads'- - understanding - - of some people but bear with me.

"Each soul is now free on a greater level than ever before to experience and express its True State. And each soul is now experiencing greater states of awareness whether during waking hours or sleep so pay attention to dreams for they often hold the key to increased awareness and offer a heads-up for things to come.

"Each soul, as noted before (in previous channels), has more opportunities and contracts than it can ever fulfill but it is with the greatest of respect that we in other realms watch as many humans now fulfill as many contracts as possible. Yet allow me to note, the need to fulfill contracts is no longer necessary. All contracts are null and void as this human experiment comes to an eventual end (after this last Golden Age of 2,000 years that began in 2012). So remember to be aware as you move through your day that the time to increase your own awareness is here for you no longer need to fulfill old contracts that may be holding you back from doing so. You no longer need to put the needs of others before your own needs. You need only to display the Love that you are and not hurt yourself nor anyone else as you look within for all answers to any questions you may have as a human in physical form hosting a soul that is now becoming more aware of its True State.

"The time to increase awareness of souls is here and happening all around you. If you choose to remain asleep and unaware of your True State that is just fine. But please, do have patience with those humans you may know who do recognize their True State and no longer may resonate with the energy you possess as you continue to display characteristics of an unawakened state.

"Remember, each soul has its own time to awaken to the Truth within and it is all an illusion of mind, soul, and 3-D body to believe there is anything but Oneness."

WOW out.

Karmic Consequence

"Let's talk about karmic consequence, shall we? Since I am in 4-D it is easy to pick up conversations from 3-D, especially those that pertain to me. This time around, and trust me I have been around this earth life game for eons of lives, I chose as a soul to end my experience before my usual time. This time, I chose to end my earth life experience before the time of my mother or other family members who thought they would die, so to speak, long before me.

"This was an experience for my soul, to experience and express in a unique way not yet experienced by my soul. Those of you who think you know about karmic consequences should also know that in order for consequences to take place, you must believe in them, both as a soul and as a human. I did not believe in any consequence for taking my own life and as a soul I am gifted with the ability to forgo any consequence stated by those that chose to make the rules for this earth life game.

"Let me put this another way. We, as souls, came into form to experience and express life on earth. We as souls, some of us, just like some of humanity now (a very few), chose to make rules and consequences, game plans if you will, for the rest of us.

"I am not saying this is wrong. On the contrary, I am saying this too is a choice by a soul to play the earth life game by the rules.

"Many of you who knew me knew I did not play by the rules all the time. Sure, I went to school, got an education and remained gainfully employed during almost my entire life, starting work at 15 years old. But I knew there was more to life than just work. I knew there were rules I had to follow to make something of my life. I also knew there were rules that could be avoided, broken, if you will, merely because they did not make sense to me.

"And this thing about karmic consequence does not make sense to me. Karmic consequence is a rule known by those who chose to make the game plan for humanity. I chose as a soul, as the rest of humanity did, to experience and express uniquely while in form on earth. I did this well as a human form. And now, as a soul I am aware that in order to become more in tune with the truth of my BEing, I must forgo all the earth life game rules and return to the Wholeness I never, you never, really left. I know that makes sense to some of those reading this. For those who do not understand, in time you will, whether still in human form or after your physical death.

"I am Wendy Olivia Wright and I am here in 4-D to relate that for those of us (God Beings, unique aspects of God, *All That Is* or whatever you choose to name it) who chose not to play the earth life game by the rules made by some souls, there is no karmic consequence."

WOW out.

Leaving The Game Of Earth Life

"Let's talk about experience today, shall we? As you know, in the minds of many, I took the easy way out. I know you don't think that Mom. You know it was part of my soul plan to experience what I did, and continue to experience, and that is what I'd like to clarify today.

"For many souls, the opportunity to 'take the easy way out' is there. Some souls take it, take their own lives, while some do not. In the course of experiencing near-death we are shown what will happen if we stay. Some of us choose to stay while others choose to leave and return when conditions are more to our soul's liking. This is not often an easy choice for some of us have to start with a fresh experience of not knowing who we are or why we are on earth.

"Each soul chooses its experience before coming into form and that experience includes many more so called contracts than we can possibly fulfill in one lifetime. This gives us plenty of opportunity to experience and express and plenty of options to compensate for our free will choices along the way.

"I know many of you on earth are aware of this but many people are not and so I will continue to share what I know as it becomes time for each sharing. Well that is it for today. I do hope this was helpful to those of you who seek this kind of information.

"Know that when it is your time to leave the physical plane, you will be given options. Choose wisely, based upon what you wish to experience and know it really makes no difference in the grand scheme of things. For this is really an awesome game we as souls chose to play to learn that we are not separate at all."

WOW out.

Life After Death

"Life after death is not the picnic I thought it would be. As souls, we come into bodily form to experience certain things and when we end that experience, as I did, there is a consequence that the soul must face. We are faced with the emotional realm of reality, a realm where we still sense and feel the body, as it was when we left it, but there is no body to deal with as far as daily functions go (such as eating or eliminating). We are shown what would have occurred if we had stayed in human form - the options are varied - and we are shown what could have been accomplished to expand the experience of our soul.

"We are then given choices. We can choose to return to human form to experience what our soul chooses to experience, or we can remain in outer realms either serving humanity, as I, or moving on to other realms of experience in other forms. This is not a standard procedure, but rather a choice each soul makes upon coming into bodily form. The choices are endless for soul experience. Many souls do not choose to be in human form because it is an old game and they have experienced as much as they cared to being human.

"More souls than ever before now choose to serve humanity, to let humanity know there is much more to life than being in physical form. We are all co-creators with the ability to manifest what we wish but the earth game includes a clause where we forget our true nature. Many souls now choose to remember this clause and do not wish to participate in the forgetfulness known in previous lives.

"There are many souls now coming into human form that have chosen to play a new game of remembering, of being the co-creators we truly are, of manifesting on much higher levels than ever before. We have that choice as well but it is not something I choose to do at this time. My current soul choice is to help humanity put a human face to the unseen realms of higher, greater existence and I can do that through my mother as long as she remains ready, willing, and able.

"Yes, the energy can be manipulated to a speed more to your liking," she says as I silently complain about the words coming faster than I can type.

"We are done communicating for today. Just be aware; humanity, you will have many choices when you leave your human form. Choose wisely."

WOW out.

Life Disturbances

Rain continues to fall from gray Florida skies as my computer malfunctions. Of course, it's a sign that another message from my newly departed daughter wants to come though me. When my son transitioned nearly twelve years ago, I learned rather quickly that if I did not stop working to listen, and record a message, the computer would continue to malfunction and even shut down until I did. And so I take the time to listen.

"The darker aspects of humanity are being purged and transmuted with these rains. As all of consciousness begins to hear the Voice within, ever so subtly (some do not listen or acknowledge this Voice), the very energy of earth changes to be more in tune with *All That Is*, or whatever you refer to as God.

"This god is not outside yourselves but inside each human form. This god is not part of the religions taught to the masses but yet part of every bit of consciousness that exists in your world. This god is you, in unique form, having a human experience, experiencing whatever the soul chooses to experience. I cannot stress that enough.

"During these times many humans are experiencing things they never thought they would face. Many are homeless. Many are limited in relationships, in housing situations, in so very many ways. And it is this limitation that shall push humanity forward. First, one must be realistically with the thought that conditions are totally unacceptable in order to change them.

"Many humans will choose to give up, to not make the changes necessary for their human comfort and soul growth. But many more will be aware of the necessary changes needed and seek the assistance they need from those that will help them motor through the maze of forgetfulness.

"I am of the mind that these changes are long overdue, having been to earth countless times, in countless forms, having experienced all there is to experience, and yet, failing to complete the experience for reasons yet to be disclosed.

"We are all co-creators in human form and the time to manifest a better world for all of humanity is finally here. You may scoff at this idea but I promise you it is an idea that humanity has kept at bay for far too long. Remember, as co-creators you must reach out to one another to create. Walk through your neighborhoods, meet and commune with those around you, and manifest the changes you wish to see. It is by reaching out to those around you that these changes will be made.

"Of course, not everyone you meet will resonate with making changes to better the world. But each person you connect with will carry a message for you to make the changes you seek. Do not seek people out but commune as you move though your day. Connect with those that reach out to you and know you are never alone. There are legions of angels, of higher realm guides to assist humanity at this point in time."

WOW out.

Life In 4-D

"Today allow me to offer a status report from my 4-D reality. Things are changing rapidly for me, my soul, just as they are for those of you on earth. There are many experiences to partake of and I am enjoying them all, now that I have gotten a bit higher into other levels of 4-D. Thankfully, it is not as dense for me now; the energies are lighter, and I can move into 5-D and beyond more times than when I first left physical form. So that is what I am experiencing, a mishmash of different realities, somewhat as humans do when asleep, only more vivid in experience.

"We of the 4-D realm are moving more quickly toward ownership of thought and emotion. That is, after all, our charge here. We must master emotion and thought forms to move beyond the 4-D realm. And that is why so many get stuck in 4-D after physical death; they continue to emote and think as they did in human form and it keeps them locked into the same circle of beliefs and experiences. Now that we are progressing, it is easier to move into new belief systems and ways to function without a physical form. The longer we stay in 4-D, the longer we take on different beliefs, the more greater experiences of other realms we get to have.

"This is not unlike humans in 3-D. The more you change your way of thinking and feeling, the more you become conscious of your emotions, the greater possibility exists to have new experiences of greater good, moving out of the limitation experienced for so long. This is a new game for all of us to play whether in 3-D, 4-D, or beyond because each progression, made by each energy source, changes the entire field of possibilities. We are a whole system, all connected, and what affects one affects the other no matter where you are in the realms of experience. So please keep this in mind as you go throughout your days and nights on earth.

"Become aware of how your emotions and thoughts make your world. Begin to think consciously and know that what you feel, and think, and mold affects the other Source systems around you."

WOW out.

Purging And Cleansing

"From the deepest reaches comes the purging and cleansing that humanity has waited for for eons of time. This time includes a balance of all past lives, no matter how that may appear on earth. This time is a balance of all lives lived and therefore, for many humans, a dire experience as they face unthought of consequences, not merely from this life but others as well.

"You see, much of humanity chose to experience these times to end their stint, if you will, on earth. That is why so many people now find themselves in situations not to their liking. They are in those situations to balance the experiences with the souls lived in other lives. It is not up to you, or anyone, to determine the consequences or actions of another as bad or good but to move though your own experiences with the grace and ease that comes from one knowing he or she has done his/her best to balance their own life.

"Each human is afforded a certain amount of energy to balance his/her life experiences. This energy may be used in one life or spread out over eons of time. Most souls chose to have the energy spread out over eons of time, therefore living many lives, using little energy. Some souls choose to enter and leave the human experience in only one visit. But that is another story.

"For now, just be aware that you alone are responsible for your circumstances. Be prepared to face all consequences and if they are not of your liking choose another course of action. That is all I have to relate at this time."

WOW out.

Remembering Oneness

"Are you aware of the privilege it is to be in human form? This is something everyone may focus on when feeling out of sorts as humanity moves through the massive changes required to return to the pure state of Oneness. In humanity's current state, human form, it is not often thought of as a privilege to be human. But again allow me to remind you that this earth is the only place where one may have all the experiences a soul yearns for in unique forms while moving, living, breathing and working among other unique human forms. For, you see, we are in truth One, the same in all aspects upon returning to the Oneness left so long ago.

"Many souls do not remember this Oneness and that is why humanity is now in the state it is in, having to express itself in unwholesome ways just to remind everyone that this state of affairs is not natural, nor wanted any longer by the masses of awakened souls. Many more souls are now awakening to the truth of BEing; yet many others are not remembering the true and pure state left thousands of lives ago.

"Being in human form allows one to experience every aspect of humanity without having to taint the spirit. For as souls, a temporary state, we experience these things but once experienced and cleared our essence returns to spirit, where there are no divisions, no uniqueness, nor separation.

"What is happening within the world today is a returning to that Oneness but only after all souls experience what they wish to experience within the game of earth life. Yes, many souls chose not to awaken in this current life. Many souls will never choose to awaken but need to process their pure state while in other dimensions and in other forms of being. This is nothing to ignore, nor berate, but a choice made by each soul to experience and express.

"Please remember, even when things are unwholesome, particularly for your individual form, they are in Divine and perfect order for the experience chosen by your soul is completing itself. Make no ill will toward another as these massive earth changes occur but know, your state of mind reflects only your own state of being. It is not in your best interest as a soul, nor as a human, to judge, shame, blame or try to control another. For in the end, all humans are souls experiencing, expressing and returning to the Oneness left long ago.

"I am Wendy Olivia Wright here to remind you of your true state and it is not the state you now find yourself in."

WOW out.

Seeds Of The Soul

"Today's message is about the seeds of the soul. Have you ever considered that you have a soul? And if you have, have you considered that you need to nurture it? There are many ways to nurture the soul. Let us discuss some ways that are easy for you, even if you do not believe in this 'mumbo jumbo'. I for one have known of my soul throughout many incarnations and so have a lot of souls within the realm of humanity.

"To begin, **the soul is nurtured only by your attention**. If you are not aware of your soul, of course you cannot nurture it. So the first seed you need to plant is the knowing that **there is a soul in everyone**. This soul is carried over from lifetime to lifetime to experience and express, as some will tell you to learn and teach. But that is not all souls are on earth to do. Souls continue to come to earth to help earth and humanity evolve back from whence it came. Of course, this is impossible without Oneness; hence you have the duality that is on earth today.

"The second seed to plant for soul growth is the knowledge that **all humans are in Reality one and the same**, a part, or as my mom refers to it a figment, of *All That Is*. This knowing, that you as a soul are part of a vast network of Oneness is vital to plant.

"Another seed to plant for soul growth is the knowing that **you are here on earth for a reason** or you would not continue to be here. Some souls, as myself, chose to experience and express before moving on to help humanity from other realms. It is, in fact, our joy to be in service to that of which we are, the Oneness of *All That Is*.

"Humanity cannot evolve without planting these seeds for soul growth. And so to recap:

- There is a soul in everyone.

- You are part of a vast network of Oneness.

- You are on earth to be in service to the Oneness of *All That Is*.

"Plant the seeds of knowing who you are, a soul on earth to help humanity evolve back to the Oneness it left. Plant the seed of Love and hope knowing that all is in Divine Order within the realm of *All That Is*. It may not seem so in your day to day affairs but that is what is true.

"I leave you now knowing this is something to ponder on and discuss as desired."

WOW out.

Sheeple People

"Let's discuss personification of the soul today.

"What does personification of the soul mean? It means how and why the soul takes on different habits, patterns and rituals throughout lives.

"Each soul offers itself the ability to take on new habits, patterns and rituals with each form it decides to experience. Yet, many souls discover the ability to do so is lost due to strong past-life influences and that is what is occurring today. Many souls are lost in the sea of consciousness still relating to old habits, patterns and rituals pressed upon them by the elite few who chose to 'rule' the experience of earth life due to their own whims and fancies as souls. This is not to say that each soul does not agree to experience one state or the other. But only that some few souls chose to direct the attention of other souls throughout the experience. And those souls who chose to allow themselves to be directed continue to do so because of an ingrained habit of following the choices of others.

"You see, it is much easier to experience life on the earth plane when one allows oneself to abide and follow the rules and laws of others. People need not work so hard to follow these rules. People need not think for themselves or face the consequences of moving upstream, so to speak.

"And that is what occurs today as more souls ignore the choices available only to employ old habits, patterns and rituals. But I am here to report this game is changing yet again. Those souls who continue to follow old habits, patterns and rituals of following the laws and rules set forth by few elite will no longer face the consequences of mining their own energy field for that energy field will no longer be present upon earth. The energy field of souls who persist in following old habits, patterns and rituals will now have the choice of other planets and states of form to experience their soul's desire but they will no longer incarnate on earth.

"This is a heads-up for those souls in human form who are now changing the system by following the Voice within. You are the leaders of tomorrow, meaning you will change this world and incarnate on earth again, as desired, to continue making positive changes of Oneness until all souls return to that state many seem to have left long ago.

"Personification of the soul is now ending. **Souls are now merging with other souls as they leave human form to incarnate on earth in group consciousness.** This too is the New Breed mentioned in other messages. Souls not wishing to participate in non-personification of the soul will no longer incarnate on this earth.

"This is a thank you for those souls in human form who now seem to move uphill, against the stream, to move out of herd consciousness to Oneness.

"You are loved. You are appreciated. You are part of the Oneness of All no matter which choice your soul makes."

WOW out.

Soul Contracts

"Let's talk about soul contracts today," Wendy notes, while stepping aside for the White-Winged Consciousness of Nine.

"As the world moves further into chaos it is time to realize that this is yet another means to move all of humanity to Oneness once again. Yes, for once again humanity has stepped further away from the truth of itself, as one essence in unique forms playing and experiencing a life game on planet earth. It is with the greatest respect that we of higher realms discuss soul contracts today. For this is a necessary part of the much-needed return to Oneness.

"As with all things, one must experience duality in order to tell the difference, to distinguish, between perceptions held by human minds. It has always been this way for humanity and that too is changing as all things on planet earth. But again, allow us to discuss how soul contracts play a role in this return to Oneness.

"Many souls agreed to take on human form to help with this much overdue process on earth's realm. This entails those souls who have agreed to awaken and those who agreed, very gratefully, to take on much darker roles to help their brothers and sisters, those other unique aspects of *All That Is*, to remember their true nature. And it is through their acts of anger, their violence and

105

much-needed chaotic acts that the unawakened souls begin the process of returning to the Light from whence all came.

"This process begins with compassion, compassion for your fellow man. And it is in holding this compassion, within the heart's core, that the Divine Spark begins to awaken. Make no mistake; each human upon planet earth carries a unique essence of *All That Is*. It makes no difference what his/her role is. This Divine Spark is the very essence all have come to awaken during this and subsequent years as earth returns to its rightful vibration of Light.

"We, the White-Winged Consciousness of Nine, leave you with these thoughts:

"If those of the human mind continue to hold separation within themselves how will the process of awakening unfold? How will those unawakened souls return and remember the Light within if not to experience darkness?"

Soul Experience

"Today's discussion discusses the transference of soul energies, specifically leaving physical form. As a soul, all energy is transferred to the human form upon birth. Some souls chose to divide this energy to live several different lives on different dimensions of reality and each physical form holds an equal amount of energy. In fact, many souls now on earth chose to live more than one physical life at a time on different parallel realities. The energy held by these souls is not as strong or powerful as the energy of a soul who chose to live only one life at a time.

"When each soul experiences a traumatic experience in one physical form, it affects the other physical forms related to that soul. This accounts for some of those times when physical forms may feel extremely tired or irritated for no reason as other forms of the soul's energy experiences these states of awareness. When the soul chooses to leave physical form it does so differently through each form it takes on. One physical form may seem to die in a sudden tragic automobile accident while the other human form adding experience to the soul chose to leave physicality though other means such as a lingering illness that suddenly takes a turn for the worst and dies. It is all a matter of what the soul chooses to experience.

"Some souls live many more lives than others and do so in only one body at a time while, as mentioned earlier, other souls choose to experience earth life on a grander scale, taking in much more experience and expression though many lives, experiences lived during a single space of time. There is no right or wrong way for a soul to experience and express but merely differences in doing so. When a soul chooses to leave physicality, it must do so in each form. This is often a way to achieve the experience needed by each soul in a manner not experienced before. **All souls achieve the exact expression and experience desired to expand their awareness back to the Source of all things.**

"All souls choose their own timeline. For those souls choosing a shorter timeline to return to the Source of all things, choosing to live more than one life at a time is the best way to achieve this. As a soul, I desired to live more than one life during this incarnation. And when one of my other parallel lives experienced great trauma, the effects were felt in my physical body along with my own unique experience. This caused an overload that will remain unexplained to many that knew me.

"Be assured that all is well with my soul as this next facet of my soul's journey expands into greater awareness and service. Know that **no soul leaves before its time** and when a soul does leave, it is incorporated fully into the consciousness of the Source of all things for reevaluation and rebirth as desired and necessary.

"I am Wendy Olivia Wright in another dimension of reality no longer in physicality on any dimension, until the next incarnation when I shall serve the world on a greater level than ever before."

WOW out.

The Denseness Of Consciousness

"Today let's talk about the denseness of consciousness. There is a great duality going on in the world today and it has a great deal to do with the denseness of consciousness on earth. When we first came in, as souls, we were pure and light, literally light. That situation changed as we took on denser forms to experience more, things like eating and dancing, things like experiencing relationships in new ways. We moved onward trusting that we would always find our way back to Source. But we lost our way. Somehow, sometime, we lost our way and it did not seem as if we would ever return to Source.

"That is the state of affairs now on earth. Humanity is lost trying to remember who they are and where they came form. Some people have no clue that we even have a soul; believe me, I deal with these now shapeless forms every moment while here in 4-D. The lost souls are not in a place of helping themselves for they don't even know they are a soul in need of recognition, in need of recognizing their true selves. Now let me return to discussing earth.

"Earth is a place where all souls want to come to experience and then move on to much grander experiences on other realms. Many souls do not get the opportunity to come to earth for various reasons, many not choosing to in the first place, while many other souls are now addicted to the dramas played out on earth. This is the source of the denseness you feel today, souls who are so addicted to the dramas on earth that they have lost sight of who they really are. That is what we, many of us, are changing by communicating from what is now referred to as 'the grave.'

"Believe me, **there is no death, only a change of energy**. Do you not know that everything is energy? Everything is energy moving at different rates of speed. Well, I can see the energy on earth is as dense as it has ever been and it is time for me to bump up my service, as many others are doing. We will communicate in the future about the denseness of earth. But for now, know that it is affecting you; it is affecting humanity as a whole, and it is time to lighten the load so to speak."

WOW out.

Truth Through Chaos

"The path one takes as a soul is based upon different experiences, not only as a human form, but experiences in formless matter and other forms as well. Each soul chooses to experience and express differently in each given lifetime. What one soul is in one lifetime is never experienced again.

"Let me expand upon this concept of living different lives as a soul. As a soul, one is pure energy in a non-formless state. As a soul, one is not necessarily formless all the time but chooses to take on form when conditions meet the expectations of our chosen experiences. For instance, if as a soul, we choose to experience what it will be like being in human form for a short period of time and another soul chooses to experience what it is like to give birth to a soul that soon leaves its physical state, we may choose to come into that form. If after careful consideration we choose to come into form only to leave it rather quickly, we are not only experiencing and expressing this for our soul but also helping another soul meet its desires and helping other souls through the experience.

"I give this example to help those on earth who are now wondering what is going on, why is there so much chaos in the world? This world of humans is really a home for souls to experience and express in various lives and in some of those lives, we as souls may choose to experience gross distortions of love, our true nature. We choose this state of experience, if you will, to help those souls hopelessly lost in the earth life game. For through our choices to experience gross acts of violence or distortion of our true nature, we wake many other souls up to the fact that there must be more to life than what is currently known.

"This is what is happening today with all the chaos, with all the acts of violence and acting out. As souls, we are merely helping ourselves and others recognize that this is, after all, after all is said and done, a game we choose to play to experience and express. This is a game we chose to play to help our soul remember the true state of our Self and that humanity is not that true state.

"I am Wendy Olivia Wright and I am in 4-D to help those still lost in the dream of earth life. It does not matter whether you believe in what I relate, nor if you believe in life after death of human forms. What does matter is that you find a way to **recognize who you truly are, spirit taking on a soul, taking on various lives in various forms and formless states to recognize that you are an aspect of the Creator of all**. You are an aspect of the formless matter that surrounds and lives in all. You are powerful beings of BEingness with the ability to change your world for the better and the time is now."

WOW out.

Watch Your Mirrors

"Humanity now awakens from a deep, long-awaited sleep. It is in the best interest of all to keep in mind, your brother, your sister, your friends and family, the stranger on the street are all your mirrors. Pay attention to what you are faced with and know it is being shown to you for a purpose.

"Do you wish to continue old behaviors, develop new ones or stay in the past with struggle and limitation? Ask your self these questions when faced with something that causes a hearty reaction. The reaction you have clues you in to the extent that something needs to change, wants to change within you, within your soul. This is a time when all souls are shown what changes need to be made to be more in tune with the True Self. Not everyone will choose to address these changes or even recognize that they need to be made. But for those that do, pay attention to your mirrors. Is a certain behavior of another upsetting you? Is it your current or past behavior? Is it something you wish to incorporate into your life? Think and think again and you shall find that change is good, for change allows growth of the soul."

WOW out.

Spiritual Growth

Emotion And Thought

"Today we are going to discuss how emotion and thought molds your world. Some of you know how I lived my life, molded with education and always doing the right thing, emotionally driven, until I learned to control emotion, to hide my emotion from those who meant the most to me. It was a long process, taking many years, but it was achieved by the time I made my transition.

"Now it is much easier for me to feel, being in the emotion-driven realm of reality. Now I can easily see how emotions and thoughts got me to the point where I am today (in your world a figure of speech). Today, I am shown how my emotion could have built a much easier, a much more prosperous and loving life. Today, I am shown how being emotional created the world I lived in and made it easier to leave it as well. Today, I am here to tell you all, 'Be careful with your emotions for they do build your world.'

"Your emotions create thoughts that manifest into circumstances and conditions in which you live. Think about that the next time you allow rage, anger, hopelessness, or any of the other various human, so-called negative, emotions to rule your day.

"I leave you with these questions: What will you do when your emotions instantly manifest your world? Will you become more proficient at consciously monitoring emotion to build yourself a better life?"

WOW out.

Evolving Consciousness

"Everyday, if you will, is a different experience here in 4-D. My brother has stepped-up, so to speak, evolved further, as a result of helping me adjust and that is a good thing. He has been hanging out in 4-D on occasion to assist me when needed and I am grateful for that but now he will only check-in when I really need him and that's okay. That's okay because he has shown me the ins and outs of moving through this dimension without getting caught in the warped games of disembodied souls. There sure are a lot of warped games here!

"Anyway, today I'd like to talk about evolving consciousness, evolving consciousness to the point where you actually know you are part of something bigger than your small self, evolving consciousness to the point where you realize that there is no outside god to guide you but a part of your very own self just waiting for recognition.

"I know that may sound odd to a lot of people, especially those who believe 'Jesus saves.' But let me tell you, hanging out here in 4-D, watching disembodied souls struggle to get to where I am blessed to travel, is a real challenge, for they have yet to learn what I know.

"There are higher realms in this reality and those higher realms are part of the Oneness my mom and many others speak of. Those higher realms are part of the mass consciousness of those who know they too are the Creator, God, whatever you want to call it.

"So just know that **as your consciousness evolves on earth, while still in bodily form, so too does your soul evolve.**"

WOW out.

Experience Is The Best Teacher

"Let us discuss the ways and means of transformation today.

"Many people are aware of vast changes within their own awareness and that of others. Some discount these happenings thinking they are but a part of their own imagination. I am here to tell you they are Consciousness awakening to its own spiritual magnificence.

"Discounting something always serves to hold one back. Without the recognition of an awareness, that awareness falls by the wayside and is soon forgotten. One would never forget his or her school studies but one always seems to discount his or her own experience. As many know, experience is the best teacher, the best convincer of what is real in your world. One may discount the experiences of another but this is much harder to do when one has the experience himself/herself. That is why so much of humanity now experiences transformation after death of loved ones, after near-death experiences, or after other revealing circumstances from unseen realms. One does not discount his/her own unique experience as rapidly as they would that of anothers.

"And so you see why many children are leaving their families, why many people toil to find wisdom within themselves after a near-death experience, and why so much of humanity now senses there is much more to life than what is seen. Humanity shall experience more of these occurrences as time goes on, for there are still many who are not choosing to awaken from the illusion of this earth.

"The Oneness of humanity must be recognized in order for the Whole of One to come forth into seen realms. This will, sadly, not occur in any of your lifetimes but you will experience it in other lives if you so choose.

"Be aware of the family that surrounds you. This family is the family of humanity not the blood family many of you recognize so wholeheartedly. Be aware that all are One and each unique one you interact with holds a clue to your own awakening. **We are indeed angels leading one another Home.**"

WOW out.

Signs Of Awakening

"Today's message centers on signs of awakening to humanity's true nature. Many souls agreed to this natural event to experience before birthing into human form. This is not to say that all souls agreed to do this but all humans are feeling the effects of awakening as earth morphs back to the Light from whence it came.

"For those unaware of the background of today's message, here's some information to help you understand what is being said. Earth was a body of Light many, many eons ago just as many other planets. It is now time for earth to return to that state and this will be accomplished within this Golden Age of 2,000 years, which started in 2012. Earth is morphing and changing constantly to return to this state of BEing and as she does so too must all upon her. Many cannot withstand the changes and leave earth to undergo this process at a later time. Many are not aware of these changes. This has been addressed in previous messages. This message is to expand upon previous discussions to a few particular signs of awakening.

"First there's the ear ringing. Yes, **ear ringing can be a sign of awakening**, especially for those with constant tones in their left ear, as higher realms connect with humanity and download certain codes of information. Many humans think this is a medical condition and seek help from health-care professionals. This is not to say that some of humanity may not have what is called a medical condition but only a heads-up to let you know that not all ear ringing is the result of a human deformity diagnosed by the health care system.

"Another condition many humans have trouble dealing with is connecting to other realms. Yes, the veils are thinning and **humanity is now much more able to access other dimensions not only while asleep but more so in the daytime**. Of course, first the 4-D realm of reality becomes more visible to certain humans and as this occurs many people may feel uneasy, become psychotic, from 4-D attachments. It is with a great deal of caution that I, Wendy Olivia Wright, relay this information. Some people allow their aura to become open, torn, defective, if you will and when this happens along with heightened intuition, this can become more cumbersome. For many humans sense these energies, allow them, unknowingly to channel through them, and become lost in their own reality. Their own life and reality is then replaced with that of these energies from the 4-D realm. This is not a pleasant experience.

"Mom is becoming nervous as she tries to step aside for me to relate this but I want to make one thing clear before this message ends. I did not want or desire to leave my physical form but when certain things happened to me, certain things I could not understand related to awakening, I lost all sense of reality at one point. This is not easy for Mom to disclose but I wish it to be known to help others." (Wendy had very heightened intuition and often told me to 'walk with one foot in both worlds.' But she tried to turn off her own senses in 2005. I note this in my second book after we had a duplicate dream of her brother while at a conference in Manhattan, New York.)

"Please, if you are having any changes in how you relate to life, any ear ringing, any voices that seem to speak to you at all hours of the day and night, before you place your peace of mind, your body and your life in the hands of the medical system, sit back. Focus on your heart and ask, 'Is this coming from the real me?' Ask people who appear to be tuned into a greater sense of spiritual reality for information on these subjects, search the internet for information and know you are not the only one feeling and experiencing these signs of awakening.

"Intuition heightens as we reach a certain stage in our development and when we couple that increased intuition with tears in auras and 4-D communication, it can wreck havoc in our lives."

WOW out.

States Of Awareness

"Let us discuss the reality of your awareness today, shall we Mom? You may be wondering exactly what I mean by 'the reality of your awareness' or you may understand that the term means your reality is based on your awareness. Let us take this step by step, shall we?

"The reality of your awareness is always based on what state of awareness/mind/emotional state you are in tune with on a momentary basis. Let us say for instance that you are feeling a bit tired. You have had a long day and are now feeling it is time to go to bed because the clock notes it is bedtime. But what if there was no clock? What if there was nothing to remind you of what kind of day you had or what time it was? Do you think your awareness would change?

"Indeed, it would. For you see, each human bases their state of living on his or her awareness. And by that, I mean **each moment of your life is guided by preconceived thoughts, dependent on emotions, dependent on habits, dependent on daily rituals of living**.

"But what if you allowed your awareness to expand, to increase its state to a fuller way of feeling and thinking? In this instance (the one above) you would not know time nor recall you had a long day. In this state of awareness, you would allow yourself to continue the time you have doing whatever you wish to do, whether it be to actually go to sleep or begin another day.

"It is with the greatest of respect that I offer you another way to move though your day. Do not depend upon the clock or past events/circumstances to rule you or your day. Be only aware of what you wish to accomplish, what you wish to experience and express and take it from there.

"Yes, this may sound strange but try it and see if you do not accomplish more, express more, move with the times more, merely by not paying attention to time or past circumstances.

"This is Wendy Olivia Wright and I am here to help all those ready to listen and increase their state of awareness."

WOW out.

Obviously, for those with standard jobs, where a time clock is necessary this experiment can only be attempted during non-working hours...or part of it anyway!

Unseen Riches

"Where do your riches lie? If you are like most people, you will relate to the desire for riches in the form of physical matter, money, houses, cars, boats and other things. But if you are awakened in a state of remembrance of what truly matters you relate to the riches of soul growth, the unseen riches that carry one from life to life.

"Shall we discuss this a bit further?

"Many people now struggle to pay a mortgage that is now priced above their homes value. Some struggle to pay for two cars, unused vacation boats, and other things of so-called value, and yet, the true riches of ones life are left unnoticed, family, friends, time to sit back and watch the clouds roll by. These are the riches of an awakened state, time spent with family and friends of like mind, serene pleasures shared with others rather than in a state of hectic activity, which one lives to pay for what seems valuable.

"Today's message is meant to help one think of the most important things in life. These things are there for those awakened to the true state of humanity and the unawakened as well. These are the things that matter and most of all love, unconditional love for all who cross ones path, a deep appreciation for being on planet earth during this time of massive change.

"Think about the things you value most and consider their worth to you. Are these things worth living a hectic life? Do they offer unmatched pleasure? Are they filled with love and serenity? These are the questions to ask as global changes occur. Think of the things most dear to you and hold them close. Make the changes necessary to live a life worth living. Make the changes necessary to live a life of peace and love, if you so choose. Make the choice to change your perception and see how quickly your life changes."

WOW out.

∽ ∾

The Earth Game

A Soul Perspective

A personal message comes and then I hear it's time to share something about looking at life from a soul's perspective. Well, honestly, that is the only thing that keeps me relatively sane (my family does not think I am sane because of the lightworker work and channeling I do).

"So let us look at life from another point of view, a soul perspective. This means that one realizes there is much more to life than the physical form. Looking at life events puts an entirely new perspective on circumstances for when one does this, he/she moves beyond the egotic mind. Looking at life from a soul's perspective garners a wider view of life for all of humanity and beyond. Looking at life from a soul's perspective rather than viewing things from a 3-D point of view allows one to gain insights into the unseen realm that reaches out to help humanity.

"For you see, all of humanity is part of that unseen reality just seeming to be encased in human form. Allow this message to transport your awareness to greater heights than ever before. One does this by knowing that things are not as they appear. As Mom notes, as a human she would never have chosen to have two children only to have them leave physical form as she reaches her senior years alone. This, of course, was a soul choice and she is grateful to know this for it puts an entirely new slant on her perspective.

"Mom knows of our past lives, of the imbalances within them, and the need to balance them to return to a true state of BEingness. She is aware of many other factors that play a role in her current circumstances and without divulging her personal life, which she is very hesitant to do, allow me, her departed daughter, to note she is well aware that where she is now in her soul's growth is much more important than where she is physically as a human.

"Knowing this may not make much sense to some humans but allow me to note that as souls our lives are often very much different than what we expect them to be. This is because it is a soul's journey to recognize the wholeness within us. Humanity takes on human forms to know once and for all that physicality is not all there is. Humanity takes on physical forms to know they are powerful beyond belief. And how does humanity learn this? Through trials and tribulations, though limiting conditions, humanity takes back the power of their very own soul to become coalesced (united) into Oneness once again. It is through this process of birth and rebirth, though death and reincarnation that all humans help their souls to grow.

"Now, looking at things from a soul's perspective means that one does not concentrate on the physical conditions but rather the reason for those

131

physical conditions. Take for instance, a human that is subjugated (dominated) by another. It is only though this subjugation that one learns to stand up for oneself, to take back his/her power and put his/her foot down to create a better life for themselves and therefore the whole of humanity. As all of humanity is merely individual, unique aspects of the same Oneness, what changes within each unique segment makes a difference for the whole. That is as many may note, the 100th monkey effect. Soon that effect will change circumstances for humanity on a greater level than ever before but now allow yourselves to know, looking at things from a soul's perspective makes a great difference in one's overall well-being and outlook.

"This is Wendy Olivia Wright from 4-D reality, where yes, thankfully, I reside less and less, to offer hints of how to survive in 3-D while in human form."

WOW out.

Accessing The Akashic Records

"Let's discuss accessing the Akashic records, shall we?" Wendy asks as I protest.

"Access to the Akashic records really is a mature process that most souls are not aware of. By mature process, I mean it is a process of clearing and cleansing the human form to receive higher vibrational energies and a matter of whether it is in your soul plan as well. Yes, everyone can access these records but again, one must be of the state of mind and vibrational rate to do so and one must, as a soul, have chosen to be aware of the information held within these records. Therefore, contrary to what some may believe, these records are not accessible to everyone.

"You would not want a simple child to have access to a device that could destroy the world would you? Well that is something that could cause an upset beyond anyone's belief because not everyone can use the information within the Akashic records for positive purposes. Some humans, if given access to these records in their current soul state and human state of mind, would abuse this privilege.

"So I leave you today knowing each human uses his/her own resonance and discernment and each human knows what is best for him/her, with his/her experience and resonance and discernment. I am Wendy Olivia Wright and I am here to set things as straight as I can with the experience, beliefs and values held by my own energy, essence, soul, and it is my soul plan to help those in the lower levels, if you will, to move though the maze of this earth life game."

WOW out.

After Death Communication

"Today we are going to discuss the various ways and means of communication. Being in the 4-D realm of humanity's reality makes it a bit difficult to communicate with those in 3-D, especially if they do not listen, do not believe in life after death. Believe me, even communicating with people who do believe in life after death communication can be tiresome, as some, and my mom is guilty of this, ignore attempts to communicate. Some of you may have read her books where she speaks of how my brother got her attention after he made his transition. I consider myself lucky to have a brother who transitioned before me as he is always showing me things learned since his transition from the physical to the ethereal world.

"One of the things he has shown me is how to get my mom's attention when she is just not taking time to listen. Electronics are always such fun to manipulate and I can change the settings on her computers, like my brother did, until she recognizes the sign that I'm here and ready to communicate. Today is one of those days and I know, even though Mom has to make a living, she is willing to stop and hear me, allow to channel though, for a bit of time before returning to her computer work.

"Another way we on the other side communicate with loved ones is by playing with the lights. Have you ever been in a room where the lights seem to flicker after someone you loved has passed into 4-D? We like to use this method because after using it a few times people actually stop to wonder why this happens because they have checked the lights and there is nothing wrong. So the next time your lights flicker or your computer malfunctions take a break to listen. Sense the energy around you. Try to empty your mind and see if thoughts of a loved one come to you.

"We in 4-D are trying to communicate with you but you need to take the time to listen, you need to take the time to allow us to communicate. We have a lot to relate, some of us have unfinished business, some of us have words of consolation and love to share. Take the time to hear us. Take the time to sense our energy and we will connect with you to help you through what could be trying times ahead.

"Yes, my mom is again leery of sharing this message as it talks of trying times but I know she will share it. We all know each human on earth has chosen to experience life differently and many souls chose to help during these times. Allow us who currently dwell in 4-D to assist you but as my mom always says, 'Resonate with your heart. Discern with your mind.' If what you hear is demanding or threatening don't pay attention to it because it is not the energy we helpful energies are sharing with you during this time of earth and humanity's evolution.

"I leave you with this thought. Pay attention to what is around you and try to sense changing energies. Pay attention to fire alarms that seem to go off without a fire or computers that malfunction, lights that flicker, toilets that seem to flush by themselves. Pay attention to strange, out of the ordinary behavior and you might just be able to tap into the wisdom of other aspects of your own being."

WOW out.

Body Morphing

"We shall begin today by reminding you, you are spirit in human form. It has always been this way on planet Earth but even this, as everything else, is changing. This is not something to be concerned about but something to celebrate.

"Many of you know the body is changing rapidly. Scientists are now trying to determine why this is occurring as blood work normally seen in one manner is now in another, meaning that results from blood tests reveal this change in DNA. This has much of the scientific community confused but a few trailblazers know the truth. Humanity is morphing their physical form and this is being revealed in countless tests, which are no longer the standards they once were. There are no longer standard results for blood tests because of these changes.

"Much of humanity continues to change their physical form much to the confusion of medical authorities. Some are curing their own dis-ease through alternative treatments, of which I knew when alive but chose to avoid. Others are healing their misthought through a variety of other methods, never looking back to enter the medical system again.

"Yes, this message is, in part, dealing with the medical system, which I believed to have failed me miserably, despite thousands upon thousands of dollars spent for insurance, medical bills and hospitalizations.

"Medical authorities know of these changes and that is one reason why humanity has been corralled into a sick-care system, to try and profit off of people who do not, are not yet aware of the ability they hold to regain and hold perfect health. It is, after all, in the mind of those that hold disease that sickness prevails. Again, follow your own resonance and discernment to determine if this is true for you. Some people will resonate with these words while others will not. There is no right or wrong but only a change in perception and experience.

"I leave you with these words:

"Think not what you can do to get well. But rather, 'How best can I maintain the perfect health that lies within me.'"

WOW out.

Bringing Up Baby

"What shall we talk about today Momma?" Wendy asks.

"We really don't need to talk about anything," I reply. "Oh, that sounds like my ego talking."

"Let's talk about bringing up baby," Wendy replies.

Now I know it's not my ego talking because this is not a subject that would have occurred to me.

"Bringing up a child is much more complicated than most people think. I am not certain Mom will agree to using her as an example but that is what I am going to do for this message. My momma chose to have her first baby at sixteen years old. It wasn't easy for her but it was a soul planned event and she felt driven to become pregnant to bring another child into the world. Of course, at that time she had no clue that we are souls experiencing life in human form. And she had no clue that it was her soul's plan and that of the child's to help them both evolve as souls and to help humanity awaken from its sleep. I came in seven years later but let us continue our discussion of bringing up a baby on earth.

"As noted earlier, bring up a baby on earth is not as easy as it seems to be. Most people are totally unaware of what it takes to bring up a baby responsibly. It not only takes time and commitment and love but a consciousness of what humans really are and what they are here for as well. And that is what is missing in the world today. Many people do not know they are souls inhabiting human forms. Those who do know this tidbit of important information are not sure of what it means and do not know why they evolved into human form.

"Many souls are now awakening on a mass level, becoming more in tune with themselves as souls and tapping into other dimensions of reality. These are the souls that help to awaken those souls that remain asleep.

"Bringing up a baby will now consider whether bringing a child into this world is a conscious decision, based on soul plans and abilities of both parents. For in the past, many decades ago, souls agreed to step away after taking part in the impregnation or birthing process so one parent families could survive though hardships to evolve their souls with much-needed experience. Now that this process is over for many souls those that choose to return to human form will again be merging their consciousness with that of Lemurian times where both parents consider the birth of a child before conception, weighing many logical and environmental facts along with soul plans.

"It is not an easy task to explain how children were brought into the world many eons ago, but just know that humanity is now slowly moving back to that way of conscious birthing, if you will.

"I am Wendy Olivia Wright and I am here to note, those who have chosen to give birth in previous times, struggled and experienced life in a one-parent family, are those most likely to return to give birth consciously, to help the planet evolve back to the Light Beings which once inhabited the planet. Remember, Love is the key."

WOW out.

Changing Your Perception

"Some people want to know how to make educated decisions, based on one of my message responses. You do this by keeping an open mind, changing your perspective, and looking at circumstances in different ways. My mom talks about this often. Of course, birthing two children in the 3-D world, only to have them leave their physical form, does necessitate some kind of attitude adjustment to remain on earth without losing all hope. But this is a necessary course of events for her to be able to do what she as a soul came to do, to help humanity look at things from another point of view. So let us take this example, much to Mom's dislike, for purposes of showing you how this concept works.

"On one hand, the lower vibrational level of 3-D, you have a woman who lost two children, the first-born son and princess daughter, during this woman's shall we say waning years. Most people would be devastated knowing there is nowhere to go, no one to count on for support in the manner her children would have supported her.

"Now let us look at this occurrence from a 5-D, yes 5-D perspective. Fortunately, this mother knows she made soul contracts before coming to earth. She knows this is part of her soul plan. She knows we are souls in human form and it is time to return to our true BEing. The only way we can do this is by helping everyone else wake-up to the truth of our spiritual magnificence. Why, you might ask? Because we are all parts of God, or what ever you wish to call it (Mom calls it *All That Is*), that oneness of all life, experiencing life in unique forms on earth, enriching souls and returning to our Source, never to leave again. This is what gives her hope and meaning through the loss of her beloved children

"Let us give you another example. Say, for instance, you are experiencing medical diseases/body malfunctions. They may be small compared to some people, body aches and pains, ear ringing and headaches, times of overheating and then feeling cold, exhaustion, and other small things. Many people think of dealing with these occurrences in a 3-D manner. They are trained to run to their doctor or seek some kind of medical advice from the 'system.' Some people, on a different vibrational level with more open minds, may seek alternative methods to deal with these body occurrences. Still others, those more firmly rooted in 5-D reality, will know/believe these things are part of the morphing of DNA, returning the body to a crystalline form as opposed to the carbon-based form humanity now houses.

"There is no right or wrong belief for everything is merely a matter of experience, so you get to choose your own experience by changing, or not, your perception. One way to decide which perception to believe is to follow your joy. You can't go wrong with following what makes you happy. Now in the case of body malfunctions, (Mom is making me add a disclaimer here) there may be circumstances where one may wish to seek medical attention if only to determine that nothing is really wrong. But I have found that it does not matter whether the body is morphing or you believe a medical condition exists. Why? Because everything is energy and humanity has a greed-filled sick care system that builds around the energy that something is wrong.

"Remember, we feed energy with our emotions and thoughts. For those who question this point of view, check the statistics, check to see when the incidence of certain so-called diseases began to increase. Was it after insurance companies began their 'Wellness Programs' where they perform yearly exams to look for disease? You will learn some very interesting facts once you become familiar with the concept that energy is morphed by constant reminders. Think and choose again."

WOW out.

Conscious Breathing

Once again, this beautiful soul, last known as my loving daughter, amazes me with a short but very powerful message!

"Every breath you take creates a wave in the energetic field around you. This becomes important when you are conscious enough to know that these waves of energy cascade throughout not only your energy field but that of others as well. Be assured when I relate, your field is solely your own. But the field of other people's energy also cascades out into the atmosphere. So now, if you are following along, you get the drift of what I am about to say.

"Each breath you take makes a difference in not only your energy field but that of the people around you, and the world at large. Become aware of this fact and make a difference in the world by radiating love, focusing on love with each breath you take. This will be another game changer in the world of 3-D. Focus on your breath, sending love out into the world, at least once a day to make a positive difference in earth's atmosphere."

WOW out.

Correspondents For Higher Realms

Today it seems that Wendy is not around. A mass of energy that I refer to as the White-Winged Consciousness of Nine begins to communicate a message about channeling higher realms instead.

"Becoming a correspondent for higher realms is not as difficult as one might think. **First, you need the desire to do so** for without that there is no way to begin. **Second, it is always helpful to keep the host free of substances that might detrimentally affect the host** (such as prescription or recreational drugs, alcohol, or other mind-altering substances). **Thirdly, it is always a good idea to know that you can channel higher realms at any time**, provided you do not question your ability to do so. Take care to keep the body well hydrated for after all it makes the host most receptive for higher energies to come in, especially with the use of salts such as ones used in the world now (Himalayan Salt, etc.). Water is a great conductor to help increase visibility of higher realms as well but that is another subject.

"Knowing it is all one Source, within the vastness of *All That Is* makes it easy to tap into different aspects of this Source. Although many people do not take the time to ask their Higher Self - - yes, everyone is channeling their own Higher Self from the realm of possibilities and experiences they have brought forth through many lives - - this

Higher Self is there for the asking. All in all, it is possible for everyone to channel, on one level or another, based on his or her own experiences in and out of physicality and the soul's plan.

"For those who do not wish to tap into higher realms by themselves, not trusting their ability or doubting the information coming though them, be careful to choose sources of higher quality. By this, we mean, yes we as now we speak in terms of segments joining, **be careful to seek out those that do not demand nor ask you to follow their truths**. Watch for those that announce their sources are greater than others or those channels that seem to report of the 4-D reality consistently. All reports of future happenings in 3-D can change based on mass consciousness so it can be difficult to count on any future event.

"We leave you today with these thoughts. Take care to motor through the 3-D maze by paying attention to what is around you and if you seek help for others in terms of advice from higher realms, check the sources and experience of these channels. Some may be more in tune with your own energies than others may. Know that what you resonate with using your heart may not always match with what you discern with your mind. But **using your sixth sense will always light the way**, that being how you feel after connecting fully with your Divine spark within.

"It is with the greatest pleasure that we address those in the 3-D reality and we are here to help as desired. Yes, we are the White-Winged Consciousness of Nine here to assist."

Differences In People

"Did you ever wonder about weed killer? Well I have. Yes, I know it is an unusual question but it got your attention didn't it? And now that I have your attention, I'd like to talk about the differences in people today.

"You see, humanity has devised this grand earth game to play to help our souls recognize that we are not separate, that we are not humans, that we are, indeed, the same, a part of the Oneness in which all reside. It makes no difference who you are or where you live. It makes no difference what color your skin is or even where you were born. For the truth is each human is part of something much bigger and grander than can ever be imagined in human form. Yes, even in the realm of 4-D this grandness, this greatness of BEing can never be recognized or known to its fullest extent. I am talking about the aspects of *All That Is* who decided to take an adventure and pretend to be separate when in fact no aspect of *All That Is* can ever be separate.

"So now that we have that out of the way, allow me to relate that humanity has developed this wonderful game where we as souls can come to earth to play again, and again and again. And what a grand game it is as we take on unique forms each time we come. Have you ever thought about that? Have you ever appreciated the varied forms of humanity? Well it is time to do so now, for as with everything else, this will change. As with all things this aspect of *All That Is* will at a time cease to exist.

"So when you see someone on the street, in a car, or on the television or internet, when you envision someone you are reading about with dislike, remember he/she came here just as you did to play the game. And he/she chose to be different. Some chose to take a stand for something no one else will. Some came to make changes by acting out in ruthless ways. Yes, when you see these human beings especially, thank them for coming. Thank all of humanity for coming to earth to play the game and know each one is a part of *All That Is*. Each human is a part of you. Each human will cease to be, never to return when this game ends so take the time to appreciate and enjoy humanity and life now. Take the time to be in the moment of now and recall some souls will never return to play the game again. Some of us souls will continue to guide from other realms until the earth game ends permanently."

WOW out.

Everything Is Energy

"Let's talk about energy, shall we? As you may know, everything is energy. Consciousness is energy. Thoughts are energy. Emotions are energy. Perception is energy. Everything is energy molded to your way of thinking. Everything is energy brought into form through emotion, feelings, which create thoughts that create physical manifestations in your world. Everything is energy molded to the perfection of your own thoughts. So it's important to know how this energy gets molded.

"Let us take this step by step, shall we?

"Everything is energy. Everything is consciousness. It is all around you. It is within you; it is the substance of which you are. It is the substance of which all beings on earth are. It is all a whole of *All That Is* or ever will be. *All That Is* or ever will be is the sum total of everything that exists. *All That is* and ever will be is already there as a formless matter, energy, consciousness, if you will. This energy/consciousness gets molded to your will.

"How you ask?

"By the sheer emotion of your body, your mind, your will to perceive.

How does this turn into thought?

"You might ask, 'How do thoughts form?' That would be a more astute question.

Feelings/emotions, create the thoughts you form in your mind. These thoughts are formed by your brain. Each human's brain is different with a great range of thoughts to express. Each human's emotions are different as well and based upon, wait for it, experience, the experience of the soul.

"As you may know, you are here to experience, as souls, to experience greater and greater states of awareness, to know that of which you are not, to return to what you in Truth really are.

"Emotions within your chosen form create the thoughts that propel you to act or not act on certain feelings. Say for instance that you have a feeling of great anger and rage against another human. This feeling can come from this life, over something this person in your perception has done, or it can result from something that occurred in previous lifetimes as soul. It makes no difference where the feeling comes from. The difference is in your reaction, your thought and subsequent action to the feeling.

"Stay with me now. This is important. Everything is energy. Everything is consciousness. Everything is feeling. Everything is *All That Is*. Everything is One. Everything is a part of *All That Is* experiencing life in different forms and states of awareness on earth.

"So when you feel your emotions it is up to you to choose whether to react or respond, to act or not act. And it makes no difference what you do. For remember, humans are on earth to experience and express every aspect of *All That Is*."

WOW out.

Free Will

"Let's talk about free will today, shall we Mom?

"Free will is something we are gifted with upon taking on human form. This is not to say that everyone uses their free will once in physicality. But it is a choice that souls do have as an option when entering into the earth form contract. Souls who wish to evolve to greater and greater heights of evolution, expanding their awareness in experience and reaping what they sow, while not falling under the control of other souls, use this free will widely.

"You see, an issue on earth now is the propensity to stay in one's comfort zone, not to follow the option of free will. Take for instance, a woman who is continually downtrodden by her husband. Let's say she has three children all small under the age of ten. And let's say she is a housewife with no skills to qualify her for a good job (not that there are any anymore but that is a different message, LOL).

"So here she is day after day held down by her loving husband who sees things only his way and is not willing to look at things in another way. Let's say she has spent the last ten years solely focused on her children and she has limited social skills. She is not aware of the help that awaits her if she uses her free will and is not aware that there is another way to live.

155

"Let us now throw divine intervention into the mix. By some quirk of fate, the exact person to help her break free from the overbearing control of her husband appears at the grocery store while she shops for food. She enters into a conversation with this angel in physical form who is aware of their soul contract to help her build a better life for herself and children. But the woman is not interested in anything the person has to say that moves her out of the comfort zone of having a steady circumstance in which to live. She is offered a choice but chooses to ignore her free will, not knowing that freedom from the soul now known as her husband would not only assist in her evolution but that of her children as well.

"It is easy to ignore free will when you are fearful of change and that is what is happening today all over the world. So allow me to note, change, as many now know, is the only thing you can count on. So if you are in limited circumstances and a human angel offers another way to live, a way out of the limitation experienced for far too long, consider putting fear aside to at least evaluate the options discovered though common conversation.

"This is Wendy Olivia Wright and I am here to note, free will is available to all and not just a few. Free will is the greatest gift humanity has to free its self from limiting conditions."

WOW out.

Grounding

"Let's talk about grounding today. As these massive energies continue to come into earth's atmosphere, it is vital to ground yourself daily to withstand them. Many people do not know this or do not take the time to ground themselves and that is one of the reasons that they experience physical disease.

"Grounding yourself is easy if you know what to do. It can be as simple as taking a walk outside, breathing the air and interacting with nature. It can be as simple as merely sitting on the ground. It can be as easy as knowing you must drink lots of pure water. Many others ways help one to ground but the point is that it must be done.

"And speaking of grounding, for those that channel messages (you know who you are) it is also important to ground these messages as well. You do this by writing them down or recording them into a recorder. You do this by paying attention and inviting the higher realms in to interact with you. Not every soul agreed to channel during this lifetime but for those who do please remember to ground what you hear by at least writing or recording messages, if not sharing them with others.

"I am Wendy Olivia Wright and I am here in 4-D, albeit a short time, to assist as called upon. Each soul has its own journey and I am evolving through my journey while taking on tasks on other realms. It is with great pleasure that I do so and reside less and less in the 4-D realm of existence."

WOW out.

Human Treasures

"Beauty is all around you. You need only to take the time to see it. That is the reason for my message today, the lack of taking time to treasure those small moments of beauty in everyday life. Don't get me wrong, I did appreciate the small things in life while in physical form but now as a formless BEing, I realize there was so much more to appreciate. Just the movement of waking in the morning is a thing of beauty, of opening your eyes to see you have life in a form and you can do whatever you want to make the life you wish.

"I made the life I wanted and although it was not as expected there were many enjoyable moments. Yet, there were many times not appreciated because I did not take the time to savor the moment. As a full-time working mother, there were just not enough moments in the day. Yes, there were times I took for myself to enjoy with friends but sometimes they too were not appreciated fully and there was never enough time to do all the things I wanted to in physical form.

"This is a message for those still in human form. Treasure the small moments in your life. Appreciate the people in your life and know they are there for a reason. Take the time to relish in the moment of now, thanking the universe for having a physical form, being able to breathe, being able to talk, being able to do all the things

you do. And know in physical form it is the only
time in a soul's existence that these moments can
be savored because once you are out of physical
form there are no more physical moments to
treasure."

WOW out.

Injustice

"Let's talk about the injustice in the world today, shall we? Many people are now channeling the words of someone who they have never met, channeling these words that come into their head. Does anyone ever stop to think about where these words come from? For my mom, they come from, on one level, her daughter who took her own life in December 2015. On another level, yes for those of you who are more aware of the Oneness in which all reside, Mom channels higher aspects of herself. But channeling me seems to get the attention of more people. Funny huh?

"People would rather remain stuck in a 3-D, 4-D mode of thinking than realize there is no we, no us, no them. People would rather believe, on some level, there is something outside them and that is the injustice I wish to address today. For it is an injustice to believe that there are many when there is only one, yes, in which we live, and move and have our BEing.

"Sure, as unique aspects of that Oneness we decided to experience and express many lives in human form. And we needed a soul to keep track of all those expressions to finally, at some point, come into balance. And that is what many humans are doing now, coming into balance, balancing all those lives and getting rid of anything that stops their total recognition of the Oneness of which we are.

"When you think of injustice, think of taking the time to recognize the Oneness all around you. Seek not to fix something outside yourself but seek only to fix what you need within yourself to recognize you are complete on your own. There is nothing outside you. You don't need me to tell you that and you certainly don't need the messages of those who try to trick you into thinking they channel anything but their own Higher Self. This is not the injustice I now address but something more, an injustice to not recognize the trueness of each unique expression of *All That Is*."

WOW out.

Internal Dialogue

"What is the advantage of directing internal dialogue? Furthermore, can internal dialogue be directed? And what is this mysterious internal dialogue?

"Internal dialogue within every human form is merely a mix of what occurs during normal brain activity inter-spliced with messages from one's Self in other lives, other forms of experience as a soul. If one is conscious enough, one can direct this internal dialogue to answer questions and receive guidance when needed. The issue (Of course there are always issues in 3-D aren't there?) is that one must be able to distinguish among the various sources of internal dialogue to benefit from it.

"As one who could no longer distinguish among the many sources of internal dialogue, I am here now in 4-D to tell you it can be done and one need only believe in his/her own ability to receive messages from other aspects of one's Self. My experiences on earth are vast after having hundreds of lives, dare I say, thousands of lives. And you should know you as well have experienced thousands of lives, in various forms, on various planets in both formless and form matter. We are among those that hold a degree, so to speak, of morphing our essence into a variety of forms and formless BEingness to experience and

163

express that which needed to be experienced and expressed but only by our soul.

"Now, concerning the inner dialogue within each human, it is vital for one to distinguish the source of that inner dialogue. Does the inner dialogue direct you to harm yourself or another? If so, it can be an experience in previous lifetimes rearing its ugly head to experience more of the same experienced in a past life, or it can be a disembodied entity corrupting your aura. As in my case, if you are susceptible to these types of manipulation it is easily done when one allows their aura to become dense and filled with tears and holes. This happens when one does not pay attention to what they take into or upon their body; this happens when one is not yet able to think for themselves due to taking certain non or prescription drugs. This happens when one chooses on a soul level to experience taking on other thought forms while in 3-D. This happens all the time in the atmosphere of earth. And this is something that many people are not aware of.

"How can you protect yourself from a tainted inner dialogue, you may ask? Take the time to check in with yourself on a daily basis. Ask, and I know it may seem odd for many people, 'Am I the only one in this human form? Am I the only influence in this form? Am I being led to do things that are not of this form's nature?' This should give you a clue as to whether you need to cleanse your aura.

"You can cleanse your aura by fasting and eating a diet of whole foods, rich in organic matter. You can cleanse your human form by bathing in Epsom salts and you can cleanse your form by doing any number of things, which one can learn though avenues such as the internet or others who teach such things.

"The point today is that inner dialogue occurs within every human being and it is up to each human to determine if he/she is in charge of his/her own thought system. Being in charge of your own thought system is vital during this time of massive change. Being in charge of your own thought system is the only thing that will get you though this maze of 3-D and 4-D referred to as human life."

WOW out.

Life On Earth

"Life is not all it is cracked up to be. By this, I mean that life on earth is not what anyone believes it to be at all. Life on earth is an experiment in knowing, an awareness of the essence of one's True Self, experiencing life in physicality, if only for a short time. This earth life is, as many know, yet one of many, many lives in physicality, all with its own experiences, expressions, and loves to deal with, all with its dramas, uncertainties and laughter, all with its joys and blessings, all with its love of *All There Is*, as yet unrecognized.

"Earth life is a circus, so to speak, a time of great frivolity, a time of blessing all who pass through one's life with the opportunity to make a difference in it, no matter how great or small. And this is today's subject, making a difference in the lives of those who pass through your own.

"There are many ways in which you can make a difference in the lives of others. Some of these ways include communicating, participating in another's life and some include ignoring, either consciously or unconsciously, those who pass through our life. Yes, as souls, we make many more contracts than we can possibly fulfill in any life, no matter how long that life may be. But the crux of this message is:

"Pay attention to those who are in your life for they are there for a reason. Pay attention to those who chose not to be in your life for they too play a role in your soul's experience and expression. Pay attention to those whom you chose to exclude out of your life, especially those who make a strong reaction spring forth, for those are the ones you need to learn from. Those human forms, those beloved souls, are the very tools you chose as a soul to help you through the experiences and expressions that will result in the most soul growth for you both. Pay attention to what is and what is not in your life, for it is your soul's plan to lead you further toward that self-mastery you as a soul came to experience.

"That's it."

WOW out.

Living Within Distractions

As this message came through, a small plane circled above the entire time. I'm now looking for the local Ben & Jerry's that has free ice cream until 8:00 pm!

"How can we appreciate living in the present moment when we keep dwelling in the past? This is the issue of many in physical form, including my mother. Today we know that living in the present moment is the only way to exist for when we dwell on the past, what happened, what could have been, we stop our self from recognizing the beauty of each present moment.

"So how can we live in the present moment? It is a clear matter of choice. We choose to live in the present moment by appreciating each precious moment and stopping our selves from dwelling in the past. This is easily done by careful monitoring of thought. Each thought bears an energy signature. Each thought results in a subsequent action, reaction or response. Each thought can carry the thinker to the past, the present or the future.

"It is only in the present moment that we are able to withstand daily pressures. It is only in the present moment that we are able to hone our senses and filter out distractions. And that is what this is all about. We are here during these times of unprecedented distractions to learn how to filter them out. 'How?' you might ask. By being within them, by living within the very distractions we must learn to filter out. For it is only by living within distractions that one learns to live with them and yet filter them out.

"For instance, take the example of people who have lived in New York for their entire lives. Many of these people are uncomfortable in areas of silence to the point where they bring some kind of audio device to mimic their hometown, a mix of traffic, sirens, and everyday distractions to help them feel at home so sleep comes easily.

"Yes, it is through living within distractions that one finds the daring to trust and move beyond the course of events to create a stillness within one's self. It is by living within the distractions that one learns the whole of silence is within waiting to be tapped into and explored. Live within the distractions to be able to live within each present moment for soon distractions will rule the day."

WOW out.

Look For Similarities

"Separation, the thought of separation, is merely in the mind of humans. In truth, there is no separation but, as souls, all of humanity came to experience this grand game appearing to be separate from one another. So today, I am asking you to look at those around you and see your similarities.

"There may be little similarities at first look but upon closer inspection you will see similarities in each human who catches your attention. This is true no matter where you are and no matter who it is that catches your attention. Everyone resonates with everyone else on some kind of basis. Take for instance, the homeless woman on the street. When you see her, you may be thankful for your job, your family, your friends and think there are no similarities. But upon closer inspection, you will discover a part of you too knows without that job, those friends, and family you could also be homeless. Look at her with respect now and thank her, if only in your mind for pointing out your blessings.

"Each human carries a certain type of energy and it is that energy which attracts other humans. Humans act as mirrors for one another and you may find someone totally different from you in appearance but yet with circumstances that match your own. You may also find other humans who look as you, carry the same stance, the same yearning, the same look of sadness upon their faces. You may come across humans who dance in the streets wishing you had not given away your spontaneity to do things such as dance in the streets for no reason. You may see someone fighting with another only to make up with them and thank them for being in their life. You may find the opposite, where people ignore one another while eating a meal or driving in a car and know you, too, do the same.

"The point of this message is to pay attention to those people around you regardless of where you may be. Humans act as mirrors for one another pointing out similarities or differences that once were, or could be, or circumstances that potentially might be explored, or not. Humans act as one another's mirrors to set thinking in new directions, to give pause for thought. Humans act as one another's mirrors for the purpose of pointing out the separation humanity came to experience, and yet when all is said and done, there is no separation. Humanity is one in a sea of consciousness that has forgotten it is one, a merger of unique experiences, forms, expressions and activities all meant to lead humanity Home from whence it came.

"I am Wendy Olivia Wright and I am here in 4-D to announce humanity, of which I have been a part in physical form for many past and future lives, is one great stage of happiness for souls wishing to continue the earth game. But due to the quickening of awakening, this earth game is ending and it is time to recognize the oneness left behind to cut through the separation and know there is only one."

WOW out.

Loving Energy

"Today, we are again discussing love. It's harmful to think of anyone with anything but love. You may think this is odd but consider that everything is energy. Emotions are energy. Thoughts are energy. You are energy. I am energy. The world and other realms are energy. It is all energy and when you think of anyone with thoughts other than love, that is what moves out into what scientists used to call empty space.

"The space between us is not empty. It is energy waiting to express and morph and you manipulate it through emotions and thoughts. Consider the wave that pushes against the sand making a cliff. What do you think drives that energy, propels that wave to rise and wander back to the ocean after expressing itself on the sand? It is emotion, of course, the emotion of the energy surrounding the ocean, in the ocean, of the ocean, above the ocean. It is the emotion-filled thought formed by passionate emotion that drives and morphs all things in the earth, your world. Energy forms other worlds, other universes, galaxies, multi-verses and other realities as well. Energy is *All That Is* of which you are an essential part.

"Please consider your emotions, which mold your world, the next time you feel anything but love toward another human being, another thing upon Mother Earth. For any passionate emotion-filled thought forms much faster than one of little emotion. Positive emotion fuels the New Earth. Negative emotion inhibits the very evolution you, as a human, came to experience. Keep checking your emotions to determine where they fit on the scale of evolution. Do they feed the New Earth or feed the dense energy that continues to cling to old beliefs of hate and separation?

"That is what I came to share today. Love is the only truth in the realm of *All That Is* and you hold the power to share that single truth with yourself and humanity."

WOW out.

Morphing The Human Form

"Remember when we were young as souls? It was a time of innocence, of beauty beyond current comprehension, of Divine Love for all. It was a time of great joy and abundance, for all forms, and it was a time that will come again as soon as humanity moves through its current process.

"Humanity is now as a caterpillar morphing to a butterfly. Only this butterfly form is familiar, a form lost many millions of lives ago through deceit and denial of humanity's true nature. It is now possible to regain that freedom of the soul as humanity morphs its form back, as each individual soul morphs its form back on its own timeline, to the age of innocence from which we began.

"This morphing, although occurring in all unique forms of humanity, is felt most strongly in those who agreed as souls to be the forerunners, if you will, to be the ones to accomplish this feat before the masses. This morphing is causing some alarm in those who are unaware of what is occurring. And this morphing will result in many humans leaving the planet to fulfill their task of morphing while in yet another unique human form.

"I am one of those that chose to be one of the last forms as humans to morph but in the meantime I am one of many souls who guide humanity, in various ways, from other dimensions. We are mainly in the 4-D reality but some of us reside within nearby realities where we are allowed to travel back and forth between dimensions to help as desired and needed. It is with the greatest honor that we do this joyful task to help our brothers and sisters of Light, for all humanity stems from Light and shall, eventually, return to Light.

"This is for those who are knowingly morphing their forms now. Some of you shall accomplish this task in your lifetime while others will not but chose to go through the process in the current lifetime to gain the experience for those to follow.

"I know this may be confusing for those who are not familiar with this concept but allow me to say: 'We of other realms are here to help all those in the 3-D reality as desired. You need only call upon us until you are able and willing to tap into your own source of truth, your heart space where all answers reside.'

"I am Wendy Olivia Wright, here in 4-D to help as many as desire my assistance and I am not an illusion to those that desire my help. And yet, as many know, all is illusion in the realms of mind/body reality."

WOW out.

Nature

"Let's talk about Nature today, shall we? Nature in beginning earth times was pure and limitless in all things good. The requirements of maintaining pristine Nature were met easily by its inhabitants. Necessities to maintain Nature are all the things needed for clean environments where living things are allowed to grow without destruction, without limitation or making something into what it is not (genetically modifying, etc.). In pristine times, Nature was open for all living things to nourish and grow unabandoned. But that is not what is happening today, now is it?

"Within this golden age, as in all golden ages, there comes a time when the requirements of maintaining Nature are not met and Nature is no longer what it was. Today there are corporations diminishing the supply of Nature by polluting all aspects of it; the air, the land, the water, all are now affected by these gross misunderstandings of power. Many souls believe they have control over the environment and can mold it to their will, thereby limiting access and purity for all living things. This has happened in humanity's past but shall never occur again as Nature now, for the last time, undergoes the process of cleansing and purifying itself back to the pristine state in which it existed many ages ago.

"This process will take some time in your world but be assured it has been in place for quite some time and continues. This process is balancing the various aspects of Nature through earthquakes, through volcanoes, through changing weather patterns and through various other means to rectify the wrongs placed upon Nature by few who believe they have the power to control Nature. As we move through this process, it is best to remain aware of the various land masses that may be affected by these changes. Use your discretion and guide yourself to places where you, as a soul and as a human, can make the most difference. Try not to allow your ego to control actions, but seek wisdom from that higher aspect of Self that you have come to serve.

"Many souls entered this planet to make a difference as these earth changes occur. Many are living within these changing areas unknowingly aware of the differences to come. But be assured, if you are not aware of the role you now play to serve humanity you will be soon as these changes occur in steady progress.

"I am Wendy Olivia Wright here to offer help to those who wish these kinds of 'heads-up,' if you will, and I am with all who seek my assistance, until you are ready to tap into your own inner wisdom."

WOW out.

Neutrality

"Let's discuss the subject of neutrality today, shall we? Neutrality means holding no reaction to any occurrence or situation in your life. Neutrality means having no preconceived ideas or notions about what you are experiencing or someone else is experiencing. Neutrality means keeping yourself in the flow of life, without judgment or shame, without playing the age-worn game of disbelief in the power of humanity as individuals, and the whole, to change your life, your experience on earth.

"Neutrality means coming to terms with the knowledge that humanity is, after all, an aspect of *All That Is* experiencing life in human form to express in unique ways. Neutrality is knowing you are that of which it is and not feeding energies that harm yourself or another. Neutrality is holding your tongue when your ego wishes to speak. Neutrality is knowing you are a Source system here to experience and express but not try to manipulate or change another's experience or expression. Neutrality is what you were when you first came into human form. Neutrality is yet another expression of the unique aspects of *All That I*s sensing, emoting and feeling the way back to the Wholeness it left as formless BEing.

"And now that you know what neutrality is allow me to thank you for now choosing to be neutral in the days ahead as the world changes much more rapidly than ever before. Keep in mind that these changes are part of the Divine Plan to return all aspects back to the Oneness and Wholeness it left only in the experience and expression as human forms.

"We are with you now, those unseen aspects of *All That Is*, formless, and able and willing to help those humans who seek our assistance. And we are ready to guide as you desire so ask and it shall be given to you, as unique aspects and as humanity in mass. We are ready to address many issues of your world with you if you only allow us to enter your conscious field of awareness. We are THAT of which *It* is and we are parts of you as well.

"Know in the days ahead things are perfect in every way even if they do not appear so.

"I am Wendy Olivia Wright and I am an aspect of *All That Is* and an aspect of you as well. That is the We Consciousness humanity now moves toward, being both plural and single all in One."

WOW out.

Original Plan

"As souls, we come to this planet to experience as much as we can, to be more than ever before in human form, to live a life worth living. But sometimes we take a turn and don't know how to get back to that original plan. We, as souls, lose our way and begin to drift toward limitation. That is what we shall discuss today, limitation.

"Much of humanity now lives in limitation, unnecessary limitation. We chose as souls to come in and experience better experiences, bigger plans and dreams than ever before and to balance out our experiences. I am not discussing those souls who chose to come into human form and balance their lives through a life of limitation, but those souls who lose their way and forget their original soul plan. Those are the souls I speak of at this time. These souls have lost the ability to care for themselves because of forces beyond their control.

"What? My mom is arguing with me now (in her head) saying there is nothing beyond our control!

"Well, here in 4-D there does seem to be lapses of memory but believe me when I tell you, many souls, as humans, do live in circumstances where they feel there is no way out, no better life to achieve, so why bother. That is the course of events, which leads to addiction and other issues taking the human form onto paths not to their liking. Those are the humans that regularly see the doctors and go to the clinics to take care of body disease brought on mainly by a feeling of helplessness and lack of all that serves the soul. I am here to tell you that this is the state of affairs for those lucky enough to have medical insurance.

"Believe me, I had the best insurance one could possibly have and even then that insurance did not serve my needs; it did not offer or give me the assistance needed. And then when I lost all the insurance, the medical, the dental, vision, life insurance and long/short-term disability, everything was lost. There was no way to get medical help aside from presenting myself to a hospital, where many bad experiences drove me to never consider this as an option again.

"So let me tell you now, the insurance you pay for is a dream, a ruse to keep you in limitation.

"Yeah right, my mother is wondering where I am going with this rant.

"The insurance that America provides is meant to keep people in limitation. And it is only one way that Americans are being kept in limitation.

"Yes, Mom, I am aware of the premise that emotions create thoughts, which create disease. But I am speaking for those humans who are hopelessly lost, as I was, lost in the dream of sleep, of an unawakened soul, just seeking love and care.

"I trust humanity will use this information to make educated decisions because one of the reasons I am no longer on earth is that I did not have all the information needed to make educated decisions. And if I had, it would not have made a difference because my mind completely closed after medical treatment.

"So use this information as you will and know I am still around. My energy is still, yes, in and out of the 4-D realm of existence."

WOW out.

Rational Thought

"Let's discuss rational thought today. The world is now filled with irrational people who do not think rationally. Let us discuss the reasons that this may be. Could it be because people live in fear, of safety, of survival, of making a living, keeping a roof over their heads? Could it be because people are serviced by a sick-care system that gives them mind-altering drugs? Could it be because people are exhausted from their activities of daily living?

"Let us assume that these many reasons may indeed contribute to humanity's irrational thought system. And what is the cure of this irrational thought? Clearly, these things are self-evident. Humanity must be free to survive without worrying about whether they have a roof over their heads or food in their mouths. Humanity must be able to think clearly, drug-free and in good health, as they envisioned their life to be when young as souls. Humanity must be free to take each day and night as it comes, enjoy themselves, and communicate lovingly, without fear of any kind. But none of this is happening now.

"None of this is happening now because the crux of the matter is that some souls have lost their connection to their Higher Power. They decided to manipulate others for greed-based lives and pleasure, which harms others. Other souls agreed, in this game of earth life, to allow this to take place; they agreed to be manipulated for purposes of playing the game, learning, experiencing and expressing in each unique life of enslavement. But this is all coming to an end.

"Not as quickly as many awakened souls imagined but it is coming to an end as more souls awaken to the fact that they do have another choice. They do have another choice to control their own destiny.

"You shall see many of these changes in your coming months ahead. You shall, as a whole of humanity, rise up and defeat, if you will, those who have controlled the earth game for eons of time. This will be a monumental feat, which shall reverberate out into other realms of reality. And no soul shall ever again be manipulated by another.

"Until this happens, have faith in your own ability to think rationally. Take the necessary steps to wean yourselves from the control issues of your past and know there is an unseen realm of help to guide you, if you wish.

"I am Wendy Olivia Wright reporting from the 4-D realm of reality and I am here to guide as many others. Seek us until you are ready to tap into your own Higher Self of BEing."

WOW out.

Religion And Spirituality

"Everything is spirit. Everything is God. Everything is energy. Everything is life. Everything is a course of events fueled by emotion and thought in the 3-D realm of reality. That's pretty close to 4-D reality too but that's another story, to be told at another time.

"Everything is a matter of each human's perception. In other words, everything in each human's life is there because of his/her own emotions and thoughts – including their soul's emotions and thoughts from other lifetimes. This is a strange concept to understand if you have no spiritual foundation or spiritual teaching other than that of most religions, who teach that their religion is the only one, the only way.

"Today I will discuss the difference between religion and spirituality. Many people know that religion is a man-made concept to keep people in line, to keep people controlled by a force outside of themselves. This became necessary many, many eons ago because people became disconnected from their own power, the god within. Spirituality, on the other hand, is often an experience people have and continue to have that can only be discounted by others who do not have those experiences.

"I am going to fast forward here because this subject is making Mom a bit uncomfortable due to what she thinks might be the backlash of those enmeshed in religion. Today's point is to seek not outside yourself, not for anything. Seek only to hone your own abilities to discover and listen to the Voice within. Each human comes equipped with this Voice and it is only through parenting, peers and schooling that this Voice is dwindled down and lost in the course of one's life.

"So if you have children, do them a favor. Do not enter them into religions where they learn separation. Do not enter them into religions where they are taught that other religions are wrong. Teach them that we are One. Teach them that they hold the power of One within them. Allow them to make their own decisions. Allow them to listen to their own unique flavor of the Voice within. Verify for them that the Voice within is there for them to tap into through resonating with their heart. It is, after all, about resonating with the Voice within each heart. It is all about remembering the Oneness of humanity. It is all about Love and that is what I have remembered here during my travels between dimensions. It is all about Love."

WOW out.

Savor Life

"The mind preoccupies itself with thoughts of the past and future that only serve to keep humans from experiencing the present moment. As one who dwelled persistently in the past and future, I can tell you, this is not in your best interest.

"Sure, I did enjoy many moments of now, being fully in the present moment, but those times where not nearly enough to keep me in physical form. Those times were not nearly enough to enjoy the many good times I had with family and friends for my mind was continually thinking about what happened before or what would happen later, when I was home again by myself, thinking again of the past and future. There were many times that I could have enjoyed each precious moment of life (and yes, each moment on earth is precious) but I chose to think of the past that kept me in turmoil over what could have been, and the future, which created loads of fear.

"So today I want to remind everyone, live each precious moment of your time on earth in the present moment. Savor those little things, like being with those you love, being able to eat, being able to choose your own destination in life. And know you are never alone for we of other realms are always with you, applauding your choice to reside in 3-D while great changes occur in all realms because of your efforts. We of other realms wish to thank you for being in human form and making these changes though your emotions, your thoughts and deeds. We of other realms wish you to know; you ARE mightily loved and so appreciated."

WOW out.

Soul Evolution

"This is for all those who are having a tough time right now. Let's talk about how great it is to be a soul in a human body. By now, if you follow these messages, you know souls take on human form to experience life. Being in human form is the only way souls can experience certain pleasures, like loving in physicality, hating, living life to its fullest, eating or not eating, like experiencing all of the duality there is to experience!

"Being in human form allows each soul to experience and express in different ways for as long as that soul has not experienced and expressed each unique way. Of course, many souls choose to take on human form to keep having the same experiences and expressions. But that is now changing as the earth morphs back to the Light it once was. Those souls wishing to experience and express the same as before will no longer have the opportunity to do so when this final Golden Age ends. Yes, there is a time line to adhere to and that timeline ends after the final 2,000 years that started back in 2012.

"Now, being a soul allows us to experience and express in many other places, forms and non-forms, expressions that you will never know while in human form but back to being in human form. The form of a human allows us to take on so many new experiences such as being a princess or a pauper, being president or a low-income worker, being perfectly healthy or being a paraplegic, or any of a host of other things.

"Think about the life you have now and if you feel it is not as good as you'd wish it to be first, think about someone else who does not have it quite as good as you do. For instance, if you are a woman in a home where you are treated badly (and you can put that meaning any way you like it) you can think about being a woman homeless without family, friends or money. If you are a man seeking love without a mate wondering where to find this wealth, think of being a man with no arms who is unable to work. The point is it can always be worse than you think. It can always be much worse than you believe your life to be now.

"Secondly, think about clearing a path to a better life. Think about the ways and steps you could take to make your life better, to get away from the home where you are treated badly, to meet the perfect woman of your dreams.

"The only thing you need to do to change your life for the better is to change your perception of good and bad, better or worse. That is what I'd like to see you think about today. Changing your life for the better merely involves changing your way of thinking, watching over, recognizing your emotions before allowing them to form your thoughts and subsequently your world. The only thing that stops you from living the life you wish to live is yourself."

WOW out.

Soul Growth

"For some of humanity the time has come to tap into deeper states of awareness. Earlier messages discuss this but I wish to carry the energy a bit further today.

"Some humans are now faced with changing circumstances to the point where there is nothing left of their old lives. Family and friends are gone, homes and belongings are gone and most importantly, people are out of their comfort zones. This is the reason for it all - - soul growth - - for it is only when one loses everything dear to him/her that the soul begins to increase awareness of greater levels of Self. It is only through the loss of everything dear that humanity, being what it is - - a physical form hosting a soul having a human experience - - undergoes the changes necessary to grow and move back to Oneness on all levels. It is only though a gross change in beliefs, patterns and rituals that one lets go of fear and begins to recognize what is truly important.

"The Oneness of all life is now coming to the forefront as humanity increases its awareness. The Oneness of humanity has been lost for a very long time, Now through changing environments, changing circumstances and changing beliefs, some conscious, others unconscious, humanity now awakens moving through either self-imposed or not so gradual loss, moving through loss caused by choices of mass consciousness, as a single human, or group as some may refer to as 'governing souls.'

"It is only now as humanity moves forward to the recognition of its true Oneness that each unique aspect of *All That Is* can return to the state of perfection in all expressions. It is only through recognition of Oneness that one begins to appreciate others, to appreciate the trials and tribulations of others as his/her own, to assist others and increase compassion. Hence, the world now moves toward further chaos to ensure this Oneness.

"Let no one rest on his/her principles for all main beliefs now change with changing circumstances. Become not steady in your thoughts, beliefs nor rituals but know only change is here to stay; only change will help humanity return to the beginning from whence it came.

"I am Wendy Olivia Wright with a new awareness that I shall pass along as desired and when heard."

WOW out.

Soul Missions

"As many humans know, the earth is changing rapidly. This is part of the Divine Plan to return to the wholeness and purity earth was when first inhabited by humanity. This Garden of Eden is lost to humanity but is returning, albeit ever so slowly. Earth will continue to experience major events such as earthquakes, volcanoes, major land shifts, changing water levels and other so-called catastrophes for the next hundred or so years. Of course, these events will not happen daily but as each subsequent change takes hold another will establish itself in the place of wholeness.

"This is not something to be concerned about for as souls you agreed to forgo these changes. As souls you have agreed to be in these places of change. You may not know it on a conscious level but many of you are holding the light in these places where major catastrophic events will occur. And you are all exactly where you need to be to get the best experience for your soul.

"Yes, on a human level it is not very good to be in an area of catastrophe but please try to remember you are there for a reason. Some souls agreed to hold the light. Some chose to leave through disasters to help other humans learn of the sanctity of life. Others agreed to help teach compassion and generosity in those closed off humans who have yet to open their hearts.

"Each human plays a role in the Divine Plan so you need not ask why you are here or living in a particular place. Ask only, 'What can I do to play my role as a soul? What can I do as a human to make life better for those around me?' That is your charge each and every day regardless of location or circumstance."

WOW out.

Souls Gaining Experience

"Let's look at the world with new eyes today, shall we? Looking at the world with new eyes will change your life immeasurably. Looking at the world with new eyes merely means changing the way you look at things that happen in your life. Mom has discussed this before but I'd like to put my own slant on it since I am now looking at the world with new eyes, from a 4-D reality.

"I would never have imagined that the world would look as it does the way I see it now in formless matter but viewing earth and the people loved as a human now trying to move though their lives without me. This earth is such an emotional maze, such a journey of discovery and yet it is just a small part of what we really are and such an even smaller time and space that does not exist in our overall eternal reality. I am talking about the time spent on earth in human form as souls gaining earth experience now. Many humans know that earth is a place to play and experience form in an environment unmatched by any other available to us as souls. This place is a fleeting glimpse of what is available to us as souls but nevertheless a place where most souls desire to experience form.

"That being said, it is important to know, especially during these times of increasing energies, these times of ever-increasing change in all systems, that this reality is 'small stuff'. Yes, as my brother was fond of saying, 'Don't sweat the small stuff. It's all small stuff.'

"This is something to be aware of as humanity moves through the coming months and although it may not necessarily help you to feel better in the moment of drama, it will help if you continually remind yourself that this is just one of many experiences your soul came to have. And when the physical form decides the game is over, when it is time to experience greater things, what happened on earth will only matter as an experience of form.

"That's it for today from my perch in 4-D where thankfully I do not spend much time now."

WOW out.

The Best Advice...

"Have you ever wondered about soul growth beyond the grave? Enticing title, is it not? Well, since I am beyond the grave, Mom listens to me more readily, ha!

"So, today I would like to discuss how too many people look to others for advice. Too many people give their power away by asking for the opinion of others. This is not to say that one should not ask for advice from others if one is in a quandary and really does not know what to do but just to keep in mind that you are the best source of information for you. All you need do is close your eyes, place your hand upon your heart and ask a question.

"Okay, Mom is making me add a disclaimer here. All you need to do before following the above advice is to get yourself to a safe place where you are not fearful or in a survival mode. Then you can ask yourself the desired question. Does that make it clear?

"If not, consider this. Many people are now in a state of survival and fear and this is why they are seeking the advice and opinions of other people. That is why the world is in such chaos as it is today. First, people must have their survival needs met. Secondly, they must live focused on love and not fear. And thirdly, they must trust their own source of information that comes from within.

"Unfortunately, people are taught from a very early age not to trust their inner guidance and that too is what is contributing to the chaos humanity sees now. So take a look around you. Get a sense of where you are in the sphere of survival. Determine if you live in fear or love. If you do live in fear and wish to seek the guidance of someone else, do so by concentrating on your heart. Ask yourself who to trust and chose a person you feel may be trustworthy. This can be difficult as many people who offer advice are not trustworthy.

"Ask your Self questions. Do they ask for money to help those in need even when they know you are in survival mode? Do they seem living only for or out for themselves? Do they as a matter of rule tell others they are masters at their task? Do they offer multiple things for free to gain an audience with the purchase of an inflated-priced product? And finally, do they resonate with you as you come from a place of love?

"Again, this is difficult for those reading this who do not come from a place of love for like energy attracts. You shall always attract the person with whom you are an energetic match. This is the Law of Attraction. So again, the best source of information and guidance comes from one's Self. Focus on that Self and know you as a soul came to experience every single thing you have experienced. It is only in your changed reaction (break out of your habits) that your world begins to change."

WOW out.

The Elite Few

"Let's talk about public humiliation and defeat of the elite, shall we?

"Many people now know that things have been manipulated by the elite few who think they are in control of the game on earth. To them this is more than a game. It is a time to gain more prosperity at the expense of others, a time to defeat what they believe to be enemies and a time to let go of anything that reeks of Love or Oneness. Some of these humans know they are souls and have garnered attention in this manner before. Some of these humans even know it is a game between the Light and the dark, so to speak, the evil and the good, the right and the wrong, if you will.

"And yet, some of these humans are beginning to tire of the earth game and know they too can have a different experience. Some of them even long for the experience of love and affection. Some of them long for the Oneness they have avoided for eons of time. And it is these individual humans that will blow open the game, turn the tables on their comrades, if you will.

"Look for this in coming months, as those humans who are tired of separation now give up control to help those humans hopelessly lost in the game of dark and Light.

"I am Wendy Olivia Wright and I am here in 4-D to stand guard and offer hints of what is to come. But be it known, I will not give protection, in the way of heads-up information, to distract anyone from the experience their soul chose to have this time around on the wheel of earth life. Just know, my family and friends, just know all you in human form, the game is ending and it is up to you to take care and follow your own intuition, just as I did in so many countless lives."

WOW out.

The Flow Of Experience

"Discussions are so overrated. What we are here for is to experience life without discussion, to experience living in the moment of now, rather than planning for a future that is ever changing. Many humans now find themselves in an ever-changing stream of consciousness, not knowing what will happen next. And that is the way humanity is meant to experience life – to not try and control it, to not try and manipulate it, but to allow life to flow through each human according to his/her own stream of consciousness.

"Yes, I realize that may be hard for some humans to imagine. But that, indeed, is why humanity is now in such chaos, because it has always thought it could manipulate, control and have things to their liking, all the time, regardless of outside factors, such as whether their way of life might affect others within the matrix that humanity lives.

"As these times continue to change at an ever-increasing rate of change, one must keep in mind: this is what you are here for. Change is what you are here to experience for after all, each soul came into form to experience and express in unique ways. You all are doing that now regardless of whether you care to or not. That is the fact of humanity that will never change; ever-increasing change will continue to occur.

"That is what I came to relate today. Prepare for ever-increasing change and be aware, that is what you came to experience."

WOW out.

The Game Changer

"Let's focus on energy today, shall we? Everything is energy. Everything is energy waiting to be morphed to your liking. But it is based on your emotions and thoughts and that is the problem with the world today. Since everything you see and experience is based upon your or someone else's emotion and thought, it seems wise to be more conscious of emotion and thought. Doesn't it?

"I know everything may not seem that clear cut but since I have been on earth in human form and now reside in 4-D, where emotions pretty much rule the day (so to speak), I am learning very quickly to focus more on conscious emotion and thought. That is what humanity must do if they are to evolve from their current state of affairs.

"Remember, everything you feed energy to only helps it to exist. So think about where you are feeding your energy. Do you really want to repeatedly talk about, feeling utter dismay, your dire financial situation? Do you really want to repeatedly note how you just cannot get a job, a house, a friend, you name it?

"Be more aware of your thoughts and the emotions you feel while thinking those thoughts. I am not saying to not feel; that is really important. But when you feel, think consciously about that emotion, feel the emotion and allow it to dissipate with another emotion of joy. You can get the hang of this by keeping in mind a memory that brought you great joy at one time. When you feel badly, filled with negative emotion, allow the feeling for a fleeting instant and then focus on the joyful memory saved for this purpose.

"This will be the game changer, the thing that changes your world. Yes, you can change your world for the better or make it worse, merely through emotion and thought. So be more conscious of emotions and thoughts."

WOW out.

The Time Of Awakening

"Today we are discussing insecurities and fears.

"Much of humanity today lives in fear and appears insecure in their own reality. This state of existence stems from not having enough of the very things one needs to exist happily in the world. Of course, most of these things are survival needs but today we discuss the missing piece. This missing piece is not really missing in humanity, for it lies within, but remains unrecognized in many people.

"The missing piece to the puzzle of life is a knowledge of what and who humanity is as a whole and unique individuals. Humanity is part of the Whole of *All That Is*, with each unique human a vital part of that Whole. There is no way to remove this vital part for humans come into form holding a spark of the Divine within their heart. While very few humans recognize and nourish this vital part of their being, some hide it, masking it with drugs, alcohol and other things.

"The time of awakening for much of humanity lies on the horizon but in the meantime there will be many trials and tribulations to help this segment of humanity recognize their true greatness. The power to co-create a better world lies within all humans. This power comes forth upon loss, upon trials and tribulations making one think, 'Why, why did this happen and what can I do now?'

"Of course, all humans move through a period of disinterest until they fully accept the losses before them. Some remain in that inertia while others begin to move out into the light of day through reaching out to others. You see, humanity has become more separated than ever before and it is through trials and tribulations that humanity will now interact more fully with one another and ultimately recognize its Oneness.

"I leave you with these thoughts. Are you moving through trials and tribulations? Are you or have you experienced great loss that shattered your way of living? This message is for those who resonate with these words. It is time to reach out and build your communities wherever you may be and in whatever subject you feel drawn to be within. It is time to gather together as humans and as souls with a job to do to make the world a more life-affirming place to live."

WOW out.

The Working Poor

"Shall we talk about the working poor today?

"As many of you know, the working poor are those people that absolutely must work for a living. They are the ones that must put family, friends, and having a life outside of work aside. They are the majority of humanity's population and they are tired. They are tired of working and struggling only to have to work longer hours to pay ever-increasing bills. They are tired of being in situations way beyond their control. They are tired of having to compromise their own values just to keep a roof over their head and food in their mouths, if they are lucky.

"For you see some working poor are still not able to keep a roof over their heads. Some people continue to struggle to buy nourishing foods or any food at all for that matter. And this is the state of humanity today as people everywhere struggle to survive. And while they continue an ever-increasing struggle to survive there are, yes Mom I'm going to again mention them, the elite few who rule the world with their beliefs and values, pushing everyone else to sheer exhaustion.

"And why do I discuss this today? Because I was one of those working poor who for many years struggled to keep a roof over my head and food in my mouth. And when it became too difficult to do I began to depend on credit cards. Credit cards paid for my student loans, paid for my home expenses and food. Credit cards paid for gas for the car and my son's private school. Yes, I sent him to private school because I thought he would benefit more there than in the public school system. We will not go there today, LOL.

"Credit cards paid for everything at one point in my life and now, only now as I linger in the 4-D realm of reality, do I realize and clearly see what is going on in the world today. This madness must stop. This madness is virtually killing those precious souls who came to live in love and hope, in truth and light, in abundance and prosperity for all humankind. This world condition will only change if people begin to stand up for their rights.

"Yes, Mom I am going there," she continues, as I voice concern over the separation issue of her message.

"This human condition will only change with the souls who came in specifically to make the changes necessary. And yes, some of these changes, some of these wake-up calls if you will, will be gruesome for many people. But these occurrences will wake many more people up to the fact that this game must stop. Those souls ready to change the system are now making headway as behind the scenes events take place. That is all I will say on this subject for now."

WOW out.

Time To Awaken

"Humanity entered this earth game knowing they would seem separate from other aspects of Self, *All That Is*, if you will. This is changing rapidly as more souls become aware of their true state of BEing and in turn prompt the physical form to be more in tune as well with Self, with *All That Is* and with all of humanity. There is not a single soul on earth now that is not in some way, shape or form contributing to this effort, even if it may be to prompt other humans to recognize there is so much more than what is revealed.

"There is so much more to this earth game than just duality, fighting light and dark, dueling others and living in other realities of awareness. There is so much more than just being aware there are vast changes in ways of thinking and being. There is so much more than looking outside oneself to find duality. There is so much more period. So many other things to concentrate on, and this, my dear friends, is what is happening today.

"Humanity is distracted from seeking the solace, the peace, the purity and Oneness of Self. Humanity is distracted by souls who know the game well and choose to continue it because yes, they think all the cards are theirs and they think they play those cards well.

"This is changing rapidly as more souls come to the forefront to report things are not as they seem. More souls are alerting their human hosts to the fact that it is time to report what they know of improprieties, of ill will toward humanity, of being in separation and controlling the masses through deceit.

"If all of humanity becomes aware of the truth of their BEing, this madness will stop and that is what is occurring now. Humanity is awakening from its slumber to learn it is not a limited being of physicality. It is time for each human to know she/he holds the cards to her/his own future and it is time to play her/his hand. It is time to be the co-creator Beings of Light that humanity came to be. It is time to experience all the best of everything for everyone and not just a few of those who think they can continue the earth game as it has been played for eons of time beyond eons of time. It is time to recognize we are all gods of creation and it is time to step up and become the Light we came to be.

"I am Wendy Olivia Wright and I am here to announce, it is time to appreciate your gifts, the gifts of humanity, the gifts of the soul, and the vast ability of humanity to make the world a heaven on earth. It is time."

WOW out.

What Is Reality?

"Reality for many people on earth is exactly what they perceive it to be. By that, I mean reality is made with the emotions and thoughts of each human on earth. And yet, that reality is both for individuals and the collective and also the reality of those who hold the keys, those with the excess of money and power who wish to control others. Yes, I am again addressing the difference between the rich and the poor, the greedy and the not-so-greedy (or at least those without the vast reach of few powerful elite).

"The so-called powerful elite are now pulling the strings of humanity thinking they will continue to have their way, continue to overpower those without a clue as to what is happening. But I have news from the 4-D realm of consciousness for you. This is not to be, not for much longer, in any event, as humanity receives and will continue to receive help from higher realms (and I don't mean the 4-D realm where I am, LOL).

"My mom is laughing at this remark! Well, joy is good so I'm happy to make her happy!

"Anyway, back to the subject of the day, power, greed, control. It is becoming increasingly evident that there is much manipulation going on in the markets, in the price of oil, metals, food and other commodities. This will continue for a bit but will cease when the elite think they have the upper hand. However, things will not go their way for long. You see, there are many powerful people on earth, many people who are making a difference every second of the day and night by spreading their Light and asking others to do the same. It has been going on for centuries but this time there are many, many more lightworkers, wayshowers, starseeds and others who have agreed (as souls) to come to earth in human form just for this grand event, this taking back of the Power that humanity relinquished so long ago, merely by forgetting that they have it!

"And so this is meant to be; humanity will be controlled by the few elite no longer. Humanity will take back their Power and know they are part of the Whole of Creation with the ability to co-create a better world where all humans are treated lovingly and cared for exactly the same, as the true Beings of Light that they are.

"In the meantime, as things unfold, it is best to continue spreading your Light, preparing for global and local disruptions and knowing that you are the savior you seek."

WOW out.

You Are Unique

"As long as we remain in a body, we are encased within our own energy field of emotions/feelings, thoughts, that shape our world. This world, this perception of a world, lies only within our own body, our own 3-D reality, and no one else's. There is no one outside of us who feels as we do, thinks or manifests as we do through our emotions, thoughts and deeds. This is something to keep in mind as humanity moves though this next phrase of evolution.

"You alone are responsible for your emotions, thoughts, and deeds. You alone are the only one sensing those emotions/feelings, thoughts. There is no one else who emotes or feels as you do. There is no one else who manifests as you do. Each human is alone in his/her own world of thinking. So when we attempt to explain or convince someone of our emotions/feelings, thoughts, or being in one manner, be aware that we are merely attempting to process those emotions/feelings and thoughts within our small self of one.

"Keeping this in mind is a good thing for those of you who work with others in helping them to process their emotions/feelings and thoughts. Listen carefully and be aware that they in reality have nothing to do with you. Of course, there may be instances when another's feelings/emotions, thoughts mirror your own but remember to use your own resonance to feel into these instances.

Do not claim or attempt to control another's emotions/feelings or thoughts for you merely stem the evolution of your own soul. That is the message for today.

"Each human is encased in its own energy field but that is rapidly changing as more become aware that we act as mirrors to point out what needs to change, be released or loved within one's self."

WOW out.

C03 &0

Thoughts On Suicide

A Message To Parents

This first channel, a personal message, came through me exactly one month after my daughter's suicide. I include an edited version of it in this book knowing that it relates to other parents as well.

"Mom, it really doesn't matter what you do with your life from here on out. Just try to have a good time and take care of yourself. You did your bit (your contract) very well with both of us. We are eternally grateful to you for giving us the experiences we chose to have. You were a good mother, a kind and caring mother. I know you don't think this is truth, well not all of the time, but you were. We are with you now and ask you to be kind to yourself, take time for yourself, don't sweat the small stuff, as Dean always said, 'It's all small stuff.'

"It really doesn't matter if what I thought was true. You know that. You know this world is built with emotion and thought but it is changing quickly with each emotion and thought. So don't close yourself off like you did with Dean but allow yourself to expand to the fullest fun and BEingness that you can.

"Mom, your life is empty for a reason, to be filled with greater opportunities on all fronts – to fill with more prosperity, more love, and more friends of like-mind and service than you can possibly imagine. Yes, continue to stay in and recognize the flow of synchronicities. Listen to us when we reach out to you. Remember; do not act as you did after Dean passed. Let go of your beliefs and do things differently. I hear you. I know you have been doing things differently and we applaud you but you are correct in your thinking; this change of thought, this sculpting of beliefs, was a choice made before you incarnated into human form.

"We are not leaving you. We are only in another form, as you know, of energy. So pay attention to the flow and step into it. Pay attention to what seems to reach out or not reach out to you. Connect with those that reach out. That is the best advice we can offer at this time. We love you Mom.

"And I am sorry, but I will not apologize for taking my own life. It is the best gift I could have given to my family, friends and self. Do not mourn long Mom; you have work to do."

WOW out.

Education And Suicide

"Did you ever wonder about the value of your education? Well I did. It is one of the reasons I decided to leave the 3-D realm. After years of education, years of amassing student debt, I could no longer get the job I qualified for and was educated to hold. Do you have any idea what it is like to be turned away from jobs you qualify for and then to be unable to work any job at all? It was the state of affairs for me as I wondered how to survive in the 3-D realm of reality.

"Education is, after all, not as important as I was guided to believe. Education, as I've learned, is not what it is meant to be but a way of controlling humanity. One way to control anyone is to put fear into them, to make them memorize vast amounts of information that really have no meaning in the 3-D world at all. That is the state of education today. People are being educated to believe certain things that are not true and will not help them in any way to survive in the world. That is the sad state of affairs in the 3-D realm of reality that I gladly left behind.

"So if you are thinking of seeking a degree in higher education, or any degree for that matter, think again. Your time may best be spent caring for your survival needs, caring for yourself and family, and learning about the unseen realms of assistance all around you to help humanity get out of the sad state of affairs it now finds itself in.

"Admittedly, I do not have the answers to anyone's questions but my own. But I can tell you my experience and that is what I aim to do."

WOW out.

Human Choices

"Let us discuss choices today. As humans, we make choices every day. Some are small choices as to what we shall eat and drink (yes, some people do not have a choice), some are choices with more consequence as to whether or not to bear a child, while others, as in my case, can be between life and death.

"As humans, we make these choices with little guidance. I am here to tell humanity there is a greater choice when making choices. Choose to be guided in your day to day choices. Choose to call in your angels, your guides, your Higher Self, before making these choices and quickly see your life change.

"What if everyone stopped to contemplate a choice before making it? What if everyone took, if only a tiny bit of seconds, before choosing to make a choice? You all have that choice. Humanity has the choice to stop and think before making choices and this choice will change your world.

"This choice will change your world because so many people now choose rashly, filled with emotion, filled with anger and negative feelings. So many people make choices without having the necessary information to fully make an educated choice. And this is the state of humanity today. It is time to make another choice if you choose to change the way humanity exists. It is time, if you so choose, to stop and think before making rash decisions, before fully knowing the choices, before being educated and wise enough to choose what is best for you as a human and as a soul.

"My choice to leave this world was made over the course of several months due to circumstances, which I felt were beyond my human control. Now I am aware there could have been another choice.

"So if you are one of those who has lost a home, a job, the ability to think and seek the assistance you need, if you are one of those who considers leaving this world by your own hand because the system has failed you, has failed to meet your survival needs, think again. For we each hold the power to change our life by continually reaching out to others. And if there is no one in your life to reach out to then take the time to seek the assistance of those near you. They are near you for a reason. Each soul plans a life full of other souls in human form who are nearby to help when help is needed. If we as humans do not seek that help we are giving our power as co-creators away. We are letting our agreed upon plans as souls fall by the wayside to relish in our own misery. And that is okay as well!"

WOW out.

Life After Death Continues

"Death is not what it appears to be; it's merely a break in physical reality. You see, as souls we come to play this earth game and we do it repeatedly, well most souls in any event. I won't say we are the more experienced souls overall but we are the most experienced in earth games and that is one of the distinguishing things about us as souls. We are masters at knowing when to take a break from the game and move back to Source, if only for a brief period of time, and yes, some of us choose to do this by way of choice, suicide if you will, as I did.

"I did know I was a soul in human form but I also played the earth game well. Any one who knew me will testify to this fact. I played the earth game very well in that I worked it from all angles. I worked hard, got an advanced education, raised a son and still found time for family and friends. Those are the things that matter, the family and friends. When you leave, those are the things you will look back on very fondly as a soul. For in the end of the earth game, the only thing that matters is how much love you have given, how much love you have experienced and how much love you have allowed others to give to you. In the end, it is only love that really matters.

"And what, pray tell, can you do with this love when those you love do not seem to resonate with you? You can love them anyways, for we, as souls, are here to learn unconditional love. And, as souls, we choose other souls who agree to make that aspect of the game so exciting and different than in other lives. So I want to take this opportunity to thank my uncles, my aunts, my mom and dad, all the people in my life when in human form. Some of you played awesome roles in teaching me to love unconditionally and it is with a great deal of gratitude that I now acknowledge your roles in my soul's evolution. For without you, I would not be as evolved as I am.

"Now getting back to death or shall I say a soul's life after death of human form. It is a life unexpected on all levels of awareness and it is only experienced upon leaving human form. But I do want to give you all a heads-up, if you will. Life after death continues in a formless state. And the joy and ecstasy felt upon leaving human form is unmatched by any other joy on any realm."

WOW out.

Suicide And Soul Experience

"Let's discuss suicide once again. Yes, this subject is of much interest to those who know someone like me who used this method to leave physicality. Did you ever wonder why? Have you ever wondered why some people choose this method to leave their bodies once and for all? Have you ever considered the possibility that the reason includes an entire village of people, so to speak, souls that agreed to this circumstance before birth? These souls chose either to experience leaving their physical bodies through suicide or to experience the loss of a loved one through suicide. It is, after all, another of many lessons and teachings we choose to experience while on earth.

"Perhaps you have never thought of suicide in this way but today I am going to discuss a few things that souls learn and teach through the act of suicide. For those leaving their body in this manner it is an experience to see what it feels like, to watch those on the side of physicality after they leave physical form and to help others learn what many refer to as 'lessons.' These include lessons of the sanctity of life, being grateful to live in physical form on earth. The circumstances by which one leaves also offers opportunities for those left behind to rethink their actions before the loved one departed. It offers them a lesson in changing their perspective to consider all the things they could have done before their loved one

225

committed the act that took them away forever from view.

"This is not to say that any one thing would or could have changed the outcomes of events, for as many know, no soul leaves before its time. This is merely to meet soul obligations as agreed to before birth and truly, there is no need to do that any longer (keep soul contracts). For those wondering what they could have done to stop their loved one from committing the act of suicide, take this to heart:

"There is nothing you could have done to prevent the act of suicide from occurring. Yes, you could have delayed the act by seconds, minutes, or hours but in the end, it would still occur for no soul leaves before its time and each soul has a chosen time to leave (chosen by the soul before birth).

"All actions are acts of souls in human form wishing to experience every aspect of life. So when you wonder why someone took his or her life, please consider the fact that it was an experience chosen before birth, an experience chosen by you as a loved one as well to experience what it is like to lose someone dear through the act of suicide.

"Clearly, this information does not take away the pain of losing someone dear but it should help you to gain a different perspective. Suicide is never only about the person who takes his/her life. As much as many do not wish to hear, it is a group effort, a contract, an agreement if you will, made by souls to experience and express human life in different ways.

"So that is it for today. You might also wish to know, I and others who take their own lives do not have karmic consequences to pay because as souls, we too have free will."

WOW out.

The Repercussions Of Suicide

Once again, another unexpected topic flows through what I refer to as the veil of forgetfulness. Try to think with your heart while reading this!

"Let us talk about the repercussions; yes, wait for it, suicide. As many of you know, I created this act with the little bit of energy I had left to use as Wendy Olivia Wright. We, as souls, are assigned a certain amount of energy to mold as we please through our own power of choice and will. When it is time, we leave despite any earth ties, based on our soul plan chosen before coming into human form.

"Many of you sense this but many more do not. And that is the source of your grief and pain, your sorrow and loss over the physical form of someone held dear. This life, and all human lives lived on earth for that matter, are really just a tiny drop in the tiny bucket of experience for us as spirit in human form.

"Yes, we are spirit in human form living as if in a physical body. We are souls experiencing and expressing differently in each life we chose as souls to live. And yet, there really are no balances, checks, or consequences to what we do. Yes, I know that may cause quite an uproar in your world today, especially with all what people refer to as the bad things that occur on earth.

"But I am here to tell you it is all merely an expression of God, *All That Is* or whatever you refer to as the supreme BEing of consciousness. We, as souls, are here to experience what we are not and some of us chose to do what others refer to as bad things to help humanity feel compassion, to help humanity return to the wholeness it left as souls so long ago.

"Again, there is only experience, experience and expression to finally return to what we truly are, One. We are part of the Oneness of all life and that BEingness decided to stop the experience and expression of humanity in unique forms because it has experienced and expressed all it can. It is time to return to our Oneness once again. So no matter what one tells you, feel into this, think with your heart, and allow that to help you resonate with what your mind will believe."

WOW out.

☙ ❧

Transitions

4-D Reality

"Today we are going to discuss when a soul knows it is out of physical form. As souls, we take on different forms and this discussion relates to those forms taken on to be a human on earth. So shall we begin?

"As souls, we take on different forms to experience life in a human body. We choose everything before coming into form and when we leave that physical form we are then freed to take on another form, human or not, or to remain formless. It should be noted that most souls, having been on earth, do choose to return to earth in a different form, based on either their experience as a human or lack thereof.

"Now when the human form ceases to breathe, dies if you will, there is a short span of time when the soul does not know it is dead to physicality. This time indeed does vary based on what each soul chooses to experience. But for the most part, souls usually get their first clue that the last physical form is no longer breathing when they try to repeat some of the things they did on earth, such as eat or talk with another human.

"Let's just assume that most humans are not aware of those who have died (not tapping into their psychic ability—that all humans have) from physical form. I know some humans do have a heightened sixth sense but that is not what we are discussing today. Anyway, when a soul cannot eat or communicate with the people it is accustomed to communicating with, it usually realizes that something is very different. These souls may at that point, as I was fortunate enough to plan, have someone they knew in their past life to tell them they are no longer in physical form, dead as a human. This is always someone they have been close to in human form within the last life left.

"Most souls will eagerly listen to their loved one and allow themselves to be guided. However, some souls, who have lived a life full of disbelief in the afterlife may not believe what they hear from their loved one and may choose to remain in 4-D, while they experience more of the same. By more of the same, I mean they choose to not progress as a soul but limit themselves to a 4-D reality, until they finally get tired of the same experiences over and over again.

"Now, let me add this...some people who we loved in our last life as humans continually keep thinking about us and we feel that tug to remain close to them. This does not mean they have the sole power to keep us in 4-D but only that for a time we, as souls, allow their yearning to be with us to keep us in 4-D. But sooner or later, we do separate from these humans who remain alive to continue to experience 4-D. For some souls, the only way out of 4-D is for someone who has a heightened sixth sense to speak with us, to remind us of the other realms we can play in, to let us know we do not have to continue to limit our experience in only 4-D.

"Well that is the main thing I have to relate at this time. You humans who help those in 4-D and help souls to get out of 4-D know who you are. Just keep doing what you are doing and know it DOES make a difference."

WOW out.

Dealing With Grief

"Let's discuss grief today. Grief is often a difficult subject to discuss but today I am going to help you understand where it comes from and how to best deal with it to remain as vibrationally secure as possible. Of course, it is always best to take the time required, which varies with each individual, to move through and honor the loss of a loved one. But let's discuss how to move through the process of grief in another way, as souls, as humans knowing it is the soul's experience in human form.

"Looking at each life experience from a soul level helps to maintain composure in the midst of disaster, in the midst of dealing with multiple losses or dire circumstances. Much of humanity today deals with multiple losses and dire circumstances as well. It is the soul's choice to deal with such tragedy, to experience and express in new ways, to learn what really matters in this earth game. And what really matters in this earth game is how much love you exhibit and how much love you allow your human form to accept.

"Humanity chose on various levels to deal with tragic loss, to deal with circumstances not in the best interest of humans, to allow all of humanity to change the way it acts, responds, reacts and corresponds with one another. Humanity chose to settle the differences within itself through this tragedy. And it is only through this tragedy, through these trying times, that humanity shall move forward.

"That being said, allow me to relate, you are here as souls in human form and remembering this fact will help to move through these vast changes in life. Each and every soul chose to experience this time of dire circumstances, if not for themselves, as humans to watch and experience the feelings that arise upon seeing the tragic circumstances of others.

"Now, moving though grief as a human is much easier when remembering as souls you have lived many lives. As souls, you will continue to live as many lives necessary until the souls understand and experiences life to its fullest. That may mean additional stints on earth, within this last Golden Age, or stints as a form on other planets.

"Moving though grief is easier when one recognizes that having lived other lives, surely you lived at least one of those lives with the physical form you now miss and mourn for. Having lived other lives with this form you may be in the position of balancing those lives through the circumstances you now face. And many souls have chosen to live additional lives with their dearly departed loved one.

"So in your grief, remind yourself, 'I have lived at least one other life with this glorious soul whom I now miss dearly. And chances are we shall interact and be with one another in at least one more life. Now it is up to me to make the best of what I have of this life and move through it with more grace and ease with this remembrance.'

"I am Wendy Olivia Wright and I am here to help as you listen but I will not live your life for you. You must live your life for yourself."

WOW out.

Leaving Physicality

"Many souls are not aware when coming here that we shall die in physical form, leave (each unique form) forever. But our soul does not die and leaves the body before death occurs. So those of you wondering about this, fearing this, take note:

"Death is a pleasant experience, regardless of how it appears to the people who watch the process. It is a lightness of BEing to finally leave a dense physical form on earth, to soar above your own body to see what you have left, and rejoice as other souls welcome you Home.

"Home is varied in its experience and based upon the mentality and desires of the individual graduating, so to speak. If one believes they will go to hell for a certain time they do experience hell but in time that too dissipates as the soul is offered other choices of experience. I cannot stress enough that **leaving the physical form is a joyous experience**. So those of you hesitating, fearing the finality of death, please know there really is no death and if you want to return to a physical form, you will have an opportunity to do so. Remember there are a great number of years left, in human terms (nearly 2,000 until the end of this Golden Age), but few in the grand course of things. Yet, you all have plenty of time to reincarnate, if that is what you wish to do.

"For me, the process is accelerating and I shall continue my world service on a grander scale. It will be quite a number of years before I return to a physical form, and by that time, the form will not be the one you see now. Changes in the carbon-based form continue to occur and we shall all bear these changes with grace and ease in coming years.

"That's it for now. Remember, those of you in fear of death, there is nothing to fear."

WOW out.

More On Life After Death

"Let's talk about life after death, shall we? When I left my physical form back in December of 2015, I really had no idea of what would happen. I thought that when you died as a human, you died period. Well, I know better now. When you die as a human you just leave behind your physical form. There is a lightness as you leave that form, a sort of lifting feeling, that brings immense joy. But then you realize that your emotions and thoughts are still there. And so you try to do things the way you did them before.

"After a bit of time, someone you know leads you to a greater awareness, an awareness that you have left your physical form and you are no longer in a 3-D reality. Then the fun starts and I say that in jest because it really is not fun much of the time. You see in 4-D you must deal with all these other disembodied souls who have also left their physical body. Some of them want to play games and do outrageous things and many of them do not even know they are no longer in a 3-D reality. Some of them are not lucky enough to have the beliefs I had, knowing my brother would lead me through this maze, knowing there is a place to go after death.

"Although I felt when you die you are dead, I also believed that when I left my physical form my dead brother would be with me, or rather I would be joining him. And that is just what happened.

He came to me and let me know, with a slap upside the head, like he playfully did when I was alive. He let me know I succeeded in my efforts and was no longer in a body. He led me through the 4-D maze to some place beyond but then I had to return to 4-D. I am still trying to figure out exactly why but think it has something to do with my soul plan.

"In any event, I am here to tell you all that there is life after death and I will be speaking through my mom, sharing my experiences and what I learn, when time permits for her and for me. This is not something I ever envisioned as a human but apparently is something I agreed to do as a soul, so know that you too may experience something totally unexpected when you leave your physical form

"Just be aware; there is life after death and we never die. We only change our energy. We morph it to meet the circumstances and surroundings to experience and express, to add these elements to our soul for soul growth.

"That's it for today."

WOW out.

No One Goes Before Their Time

"Let's talk about the changing of energy upon physical death, shall we? Yes, we are discussing this subject because I am now here with my niece who also decided to leave her physical form.

"It's important to know that we are souls and we take on different physical forms to experience life on earth. Every time we leave a physical form, we are greeted by loved ones from our current life, who left their physical form before we did. Sometimes we are also greeted by the energy sources of those who we spent many lives with in other forms as well. It is a coming home celebration, after we are first assisted, a celebration of another life full of experience and expression.

"But allow me to share how we are at first a bit confused upon passing out of our physical form. That is mainly why those dear to us in the life just left greet us most of the time. It is with this greeting, this scooping up, if you will, that we learn of our departure from physical form. It is with this event that we make our transition from 3-D to 4-D and beyond. For some of us, our bodies remain alive while certain procedures take place, in the case of organ donors, if you will. This means our soul sticks around as these procedures occur but we are not really in the physical form or able to return to it. Don't get me wrong. Some souls do try to return to the physical form but after a bit of time one realizes, with the help of other souls in our company and those physically at our bedside, that we have left the building, so to speak.

"It is with the greatest of pleasure that we finally leave our physical form and feel that immense joy upon knowing we are indeed free from the dense physical body. This sometimes takes more time than usual if we float around but in the end sense we are indeed lifted to a higher plane to continue our evolution as souls.

"I want to make one thing clear. When we seem to remain, kept alive, if you will, we do not feel any pain or sense any of the senses we did while physically and fully alive. You need to know that. When the soul has left the physical form it no longer feels the sense of physicality.

"Now to the family I wish to report, we are with Mandy; we are with her and able to communicate fully. This process of crossing over is a bit different for Mandy than others but it is nevertheless flawless in that we are here and Mandy's soul is cooperating to the point where it understands what has taken place and is taking place now.

"Family members, you will feel a sense of Mandy as you say your goodbyes. You will know she is with you, checking in on you in the wee hours of the night. Mom (Rita Lynn) you will know she is ready to communicate on a fuller level when these procedures conclude. It is all in Divine Order. Do not be fearful for Mandy is cared for and ready to make this transition.

"I am Wendy Olivia Wright, here with my niece, and I am here to say, 'Trust in the process of evolution and know, no one goes before their time.'"

WOW out.

World Changes

Today, on 4/22/16, the energy of my departed daughter comes hours earlier than usual, prompting me to set work aside to channel a message.

"Let's talk about world events today, shall we? I know, Mom, you are often leery of discussing world events because you know that concentration feeds energy. But one must be aware of what seems to be happening on all levels and still feed only those levels one wishes to experience. I hope this is clear for there are a great many souls who chose to experience certain things on earth that other souls will not experience. It is a matter of free will and choice once in human form.

"The trick is to be aware that as souls we all came to experience certain things and as souls, while still on earth in 3-D reality, those choosing to experience one set of circumstances the most will rule, so to speak. This does not mean that each human will experience what mass consciousness chooses to experience. Only those souls wishing to experience certain things will and those souls not wishing to experience certain things (unaware of soul choices or choices available in human form) will experience only what they as souls, and as humans using free will, will experience.

"So, there will be many changes world-wide in coming months and these changes will affect all of humanity, some humans more than others. This will be because some humans will prepare for these changes, while being aware of their possibilities, without feeding that energy.

"Yes, it is a tricky concept to understand. To put it more clearly, be aware of the possibilities by paying attention to what comes across your radar screen, so to speak. Even if you do not watch news or read news there will be times, small hints, of what is to come that will be available for you to learn. Listen, pay attention to these hints, and know that your energy can feed these circumstances into fruition or not. You can sense whether these potential changes will affect you by focusing on your heart. Be aware of the circumstance. Take the time to go within, by concentrating on the Divine Spark within, and ask yourself, 'Did I as a soul chose to experience this?'

"If as a human, you sense the experience is part of your soul's journey, prepare as well as you can to weather though the circumstance. You can also chose to lessen or even avoid the experience chosen as a soul. But remember, since each soul is here to experience, chances are that if you do not experience one course of action in this life you shall return in human form to experience it as desired by your soul.

"Trust your self to make the best possible decision as humanity moves though these world-wide changes. Remain in your heart space and be aware that there are unseen realms to assist you. The purpose of those unseen realms is to help you to tap into your own unique Divine Spark to be your own guide.

"I am Wendy Olivia Wright here with a heads-up to let you know, big changes lie ahead. Prepare if you feel it necessary and know as a soul you are here to experience and express."

WOW out.

ଔ ଓ

World Servers

A Communication For World Servers

This is a personal message that relates to many other people who travel the lightworker path. It prompts us to take the time to listen and verifies that there is much more to life than we can ever imagine, even while feeling totally out of place on earth.

"Come-on Mom, you have to take the time to listen if you are going to do your mission properly. Not that it matters, of course, for you know if you don't do it someone else will but your experiences have made you the best possible soul to complete this mission successfully."

Me: "So what is this mission?"

"You already know Mom. It is to alert the others through your experience, through your channels, that this world is fleeting at most. This world is merely a stepping point to help those playing the game, to hone their capabilities, their skills in becoming world servers.

"You are all world servers or you would not be here on earth. Earth is the one playground that helps souls to hone their abilities in unique ways. It is the way humanity designed the game that makes it so alluring for those souls wishing to incarnate here."

Wendy continues to hear me think and responds.

"Yes, I know, you never thought you'd channel me.

"Getting past that, remember you are here to complete the mission your soul agreed to do. You were chosen among many souls who lined up for this mission. Yes, despite all its ups and downs, its grief and joys, its pleasures and pains. You were chosen by the elders to come knowing the mission would be most successfully fulfilled, if you could only get past your own personality, your soul's chosen arrogant ego. And you are doing that now, getting past the ego more fully.

"We watch and stand by you each day, each moment you weave through this maze to control the grief you feel. And yet, there is nothing to control. Remember spirit lives on. We are spirit in fleeting human form; each form lives only for a short time in the grand scheme of things. Keep this in mind as each soul attempts to fulfill a mission he/she may not even be aware of that exists. As each calamity, each seeming bad experience on your earth unfolds, remember the lessons to be learned, the lessons of sanctity of life, the lessons of unconditional love, lessons of trusting beyond what you sense and feel with merely five senses.

"You are now moving, expanding beyond those five what many refer to as ordinary senses. Allow this to happen as all become more in tune with the energies now pouring into your planet.

"I know, you are a reluctant wayshower but get over it. It is time to complete the mission with the wisdom your personality and soul has gleaned.

"I leave you for today knowing it will be somewhat difficult to move through your fresh grief -- the grief of losing a daughter in the prime of her life -- but you shall overcome this and persevere to be successful in your mission."

WOW out.

A Message To Parents

Wendy has channeled though me for the past two days and as her brother did, now begins to make it impossible for me to work until I listen. So I stop working on my latest video project to ask what she wants to relate, a message for family, friends, or me.

"What shall we focus on today?" I ask.

The words begin to flow...

"It is time to listen to the Voice within. It may be hard to do if you hear many voices as I did. But eventually you will be able to hear the most subtle one, the one that is the very essence of your BEing. You know what to do if you have followed the spiritual path, cleansed your aura, and did the multitude of things I did necessary to channel this Voice. For me, it was a matter of weeding through many channels that I tapped into. For me, it was a matter of realizing that I was not insane or what many refer to as crazy but someone with intuitive capabilities beyond many people. Why do you think I was the person my friends always came to when troubles arose? It was because I could tap into their very BEingness to see what was occurring.

"This is not a time of burrowing into a hole but accepting your gifts and talents as they have been

251

given to you for a purpose. Many of you are here on this earth to be channels of higher realms."

"Many are here to help people weed through the realms by tapping into various aspects of past, present, and future for those unwilling, or unable, to tap into them. You are all channels with the ability to tap into higher aspects of yourselves and once you take the time, daily, to hone your ability you will get the guidance you seek, rather than looking outside yourself for answers.

"My mother and many others do this on a daily basis and many teach people how to become a clear host. Those of you who wish to let go of the drama offered by the earthly realm we all came to experience can now take the time to leave it by tapping into your Higher Self. This is, as my mom and others say, a new game to play and all are welcome to play it."

WOW out.

Humanity's Destiny

"Let's talk about humanity's destiny. Humanity is one of many species that chose as souls to experience life in a form or formless matter. Nevertheless, humanity is now moving through a most momentous time as all those on other realms watch the experience. This is an experience never experienced nor expressed, as all are, in any form or formless matter. Humanity's experience is momentous because it is an experience and expression not thought of on other levels of reality.

"This soul experience and expression is the last hurrah for the human form. This last Golden Age will secure many souls in their service, moving onto galactic service in many other dimensions. None ever thought this outcome would be possible, based on all that has occurred on earth. All realms are watching and knowing this experience and expression in human form is ending.

"Yet, there is still time for many souls to join the game and many souls are doing so in rapidly increasing numbers. These are the souls who will continue to help humanity evolve. These are the children of the future, those who know who they are when they enter human form and those that have chosen, as souls, to never forget their true BEing. These are the souls who are the game changers among new breeds.

"Yes, there are new breeds of humans now entering the game. These breeds have the ability to withstand ever-increasing waves of disease and behavior from the so-called elite who continue to try and keep humanity locked into the game of submission and slavery. This new breed can withstand all negative energies and this new breed is here to say: 'Humanity is now evolving to a space beyond their first recognition when first arriving on planet earth.'

"Humanity is now evolving into a new breed that is ready to speak its truth and deal positively with blatant corruption. You may help this new breed by recognizing them. You may help this new breed by not allowing the so-called elite to warp their minds through forced 'education'. You may help this breed by not allowing their bodies to fill with unnecessary vaccines and drugs. You may help this breed by knowing they are different for a reason. The true new breed of humanity will not forgo their True Nature to play the old games. This new breed will find and develop new ways to survive without feeding the current warped system

"I am Wendy Olivia Wright here in 4-D to help humanity as this new breed enters the atmosphere. And I am here for a short time only in the realm of earth, for it is my charge to move on to higher realms, increasing my service as many of you who now read this."

WOW out.

It's Time!

Some people know I am a rather reluctant wayshower due to past life experience and experience in this life as well. Today's message comes as no surprise as Wendy steps aside so the White-Winged Consciousness of Nine can deliver a message that pertains to those of resonance.

"Reluctant lightworkers, wayshowers and starseeds have their reasons for stemming the flow of Spirit. Many have suffered tremendously in other lives being tortured for beliefs, others ostracized from family, friends and community at large in past and/or current lives and some even leery of speaking out due to fear of end results. Yet, the time has come for all world servers to set aside these experiences, these beliefs, some of which are from other lifetimes, to declare the truths they came to reveal.

"Humanity, lost in a sea of forgetfulness, forgot that all are One, unique in expression and form but nevertheless part of the Whole of *All That Is*. Lightworkers, wayshowers and starseeds, it is time to step forth more fully to complete your mission. It is time to bring the Light of One to earth on a more consistent basis for it has never been needed as much as it is now, this being the last Golden Age of 2,000 years.

"Many of you shall move on to other realms when your task is complete on this earth to serve in

255

greater realms of responsibility. Some will return to earth in a new form to continue their service but make no mistake, your task is unique in itself and no one can complete that task as well as you can. It is the reason many other souls chose you to come to earth to be the one that fits your shoes so perfectly.

"We are the White-Winged Consciousness of Nine here to assist all of humanity and we especially wish to convey to all lightworkers, wayshowers and starseeds: you are not alone. You have never been alone and you shall never be alone. An assembly of guides is always nearby to surround and guide you. All you need do is ask for assistance. If you are not a clear host to hear us, there will be those in the physical realm who reach out to you or to whom you are guided to ask for assistance. But make no mistake; it is your god-given right to tap into your own source of truth for guidance at any time."

C ଞ ଚ

P. S.

Let's talk about me, shall we?

I am a full force BEing of nature in human form who is only now beginning to realize the power I hold within this physical form. It is not quite time to adjust that power to manifest without a lapse in time but I am waiting anxiously for that time to occur. I am SAM I AM and that is the extent of my human form. This is my Higher Self, if you will, doing the typing, the talking, making the words to form on the computer screen.

It is in the best interest of all humanity that we continue to know we are powerful beings in human form waiting for the day to approach when we can take back our power to create without a lapse in time. This time is coming but, of course, we must be ready to use it. We must be ready to use it with the knowledge and wisdom of the ages, to create without hurting others, to manifest without thought of harm to our self or another in human form. And it is for that reason that we must wait for manifestations to occur. We must be sure of what we want to manifest and we must be sure it is in the best interest of not only our human form but our soul as well.

Certainly, we have our soul plan, our lessons and experiences to move though but that is just part of this grand game on earth. We are in essence paving the way for ourselves in future incarnations, if we so choose, to become even more than ever before in human form. And so I now ask you to consider:

Question: What is it that would be in the best interest of this future form (if that is your choice to incarnate again) to serve humanity in greater ways?

My Answer: To be as prosperous, powerful and filled with Light as possible so I can carry that signature into the last incarnation.

Question: What is it that will carry me through this life to greater service without holding the experience back from its natural course?

My Answer: To not make rash decisions based on ego desires but remain in the flow and aware of synchronicities.

I AM that I AM and I am here to answer any questions you may have concerning this and other incarnations. (Your Higher Self is always ready and waiting to answer any questions you may have.)

About the Author

Sharon Ann Meyer (SAM), author of the "Lightworker's Log Book Series," is a minister (ordained by Sanctuary of the Beloved Church Priesthood and Order of Melchizedek), channel of higher realms, teacher, founder of SAM I AM Productions (SamIAMproductions.com – assisting humanity to find the Divine Spark within) and administrator of the popular Internet resource, Lightworker's Log (LightworkersLog.com). Spreading Spirit's message of Oneness throughout the globe, SAM is a wayshower helping others to learn the truth of BEing so humanity can return unique figments back to *All That Is.*

The Lightworker's Log Book Series

Book One: Death of the Sun

Book Two: A Change in Perception

Lightworker's Log :-) Transformation

Manifesting: Lightworker's Log

Prayer Treatments: Lightworker's Log

Adventures in Greece and Turkey

Earth Angels

Return to Light: John of God Helps

Bits of Wisdom

Book of One :-) Volume 1

Book of One :-) Volume 2

Book of One :-) Volume 3

After Death, Communications...WOW!

www.ingramcontent.com/pod-product-compliance
Lightning Source LLC
Chambersburg PA
CBHW022004090426
42741CB00007B/879